CONTINUOUS
DISCOVERY
HABITS

CONTINUOUS DISCOVERY HABITS

Discover Products That Create
Customer Value and Business Value

TERESA TORRES

For information about this title or to order other books and/or electronic media, contact the publisher:

Publisher: Product Talk LLC, ProductTalk.org, Bend, OR 97703

Author and Illustrations: Teresa Torres

Editor: Melissa Suzuno

Cover Art: 1106 Design and Weiher Creative

Interior Design: 1106 Design

Library of Congress Control Number: 2021902811

ISBN: 978-1-7366333-0-4

Printed in the United States of America

TABLE OF CONTENTS

PART 3: DEVELOPING YOUR CONTINUOUS DISCOVERY HABITS

FOREWORD

CHRIS MERCURI

Working in a product role is hard. There is huge pressure to solve customer problems and drive business value. Everyone is looking to you for answers. How do you come up with the right answers more often? If you're like me, you've searched all over, looking for a guide that can tell you how to do great product discovery. Most books promise a whole lot—plenty of the "what" but little of the "how." You are often left wondering what to do next.

Eventually my team and I got the opportunity to go through the Continuous Discovery Habits coaching program, which lays out the key elements of an end-to-end modern product discovery approach (the same approach you'll learn in this book). The curriculum covers how to set outcomes, uncover customer problems, prioritize, come up with creative solutions, test assumptions quickly, and a lot more. What did we gain from practicing the habits, and what can you expect to gain from reading this book?

We went from chopping and changing our discovery approach and needing lots of meetings to work out what to do next to a more structured discovery process. People knew what was expected of them and delivered more consistent results.

We shifted away from a more superficial understanding of our customers. Instead of relying on heavy, infrequent research, we developed a deeper understanding of the customer's needs, problems, and desires through regular contact and lightweight research methods.

We shifted away from having lists of metrics to increase and outputs to deliver. Now we have fewer goals, more clarity, and a focus on solving the customer's problem in ways that drive business value.

We shifted away from falling in love with a single idea and building it. Now we come up with many ideas. And we learn faster by testing sets of ideas and running smaller simulations.

We shifted away from discovery and delivery being separate responsibilities. Now there's more collaboration, with most of the team involved in customer interviews, mapping the customer journey, ideating on solutions, and discussing results. The whole team contributes at key points along the way, and we learn and adjust our course together.

With our leaders, we no longer wait to show them big reports and presentations. Now we have the tools to show them our thinking earlier and have better conversations about where to go next.

By applying the Continuous Discovery Habits, we improved customer and business outcomes, but the reward for the team was even bigger—confidence. The habits gave us the confidence that we knew what we were doing. And after a few wins, we started to believe that we could achieve anything.

I wish that I had been introduced to the Continuous Discovery Habits much earlier in my career. If you study this book and practice the habits, product work will still be hard, and you will still make plenty of mistakes. But you will make better product decisions, and the chances that you will succeed will dramatically increase.

Chris Mercuri
Product Manager
February 2021

FOREWORD

MARTY CAGAN

As the years go by, the more I credit luck for my good fortune, and the less I credit any particular skills I might possess.

When I was a new tech lead on a product team, I was incredibly fortunate to have an engineering manager who had a track record of consistent innovation and was truly committed to helping me develop my skills.

When I wanted to learn product management, I was assigned an experienced product leader and serial entrepreneur who coached me through the many major new areas of learning, drilled into me the principles of strong product, and made sure I knew what I needed to do along the way, and where to get help when I ran into trouble.

When I wanted to learn much more about modern product design, I had direct access to one of the best design leaders in the world, working on the leading edge of design for Internet-based products.

And when I wanted to move into product leadership, I had several world-class leaders who were willing to put in the time to coach and develop my leadership and strategy skills.

I thought constant access to that type of coaching was normal, at least until I left the bubble I was in and entered the broader technology world.

Unfortunately, as I learned and you likely already know, most people are not as lucky as I was.

Many work in organizations where the leaders have not had a chance to see how good product teams work up close. And as such, they're unable to effectively coach and develop their people.

I meet companies like this constantly. They *want* to improve. They know they *need* to improve. They usually understand the *theory* of how strong teams work. But they just don't have the hands-on experience and knowledge to be able to provide the coaching their people need.

One way to address this is to bring in experienced product and technology leaders who can provide this coaching and development for their organizations. This can work very well, but many companies have found that these experienced leaders are in very high demand.

Which is why the most scalable solution I know of to this problem is to enlist the help of an experienced product coach.

This is how I first met Teresa many years ago. I saw how she had been helping product teams, and I started introducing her to many different product organizations, located all over the world. And I kept recommending her because the companies and teams she was helping were soon doing visibly better.

So when Teresa told me that she wanted to write a book sharing much of what she had learned and has been advocating at these companies, I was more than a little bit glad to hear that.

I meet so many product teams that genuinely want to do great work, but they're just not sure what they need to do to get started solving real problems for their customers while achieving the necessary outcomes for their company.

While there is no *single* way for a product team to do good work, there are countless bad ways, and what so many teams need is to be coached in the right direction, much like I received when I was learning.

This book shares what Teresa has found to be most effective and will provide you with the structure you need to know what to do—and when—in order to discover good opportunities and effective solutions.

My hope is that, if you haven't had the good fortune to be coached by a strong leader or product coach, this book can help fill that gap and set you on the path to success.

Marty Cagan
Silicon Valley Product Group
February 2021

INTRODUCTION

It was 2013. I was leading a product and design team at a venture-backed startup in San Francisco. We were developing a product that created real value for our customers. It was a noble cause—we helped college students find their first job out of college. In our discovery, we uncovered a key insight that had the potential to disrupt our industry (more on that in Chapter 11). I had a partner, our head of engineering, who was a dream to work with. We became fast friends. I was mentoring a young designer whom I had known since she was nine years old—the daughter of a good friend of mine. I encouraged a young engineer, a recent math major from the University of Washington, to get up to speed with machine learning. I was relying on him to help us realize our product vision and was thrilled that, as a company, we were investing in young talent. I loved coming to work each day. And then one day, I walked in and quit.

I was tired. Not from the typical startup rat race. We weren't working long hours, rushing from release to release, moving fast and breaking things (like the early Facebook adage). By the time I joined, the company had grown out of the speed-at-all-costs startup stage (if it ever had one). Instead, I was tired of the day-to-day reality of evangelizing product management at yet another founder-led startup. I was tired of sitting in conference rooms arguing with executives about our product strategy when I was the only one who had spent time with our customers. I was tired of debating with sales reps about why we weren't going to build every feature that prospects requested. I was tired of having to convince my colleagues that a relentless focus on customers was a better strategy than obsessing about our competitors. Sadly, this is the work of a product executive.

I was lucky. As an undergraduate, I was exposed to human-centered design at Stanford University. I graduated and naively thought business would be human centered. I spent the first 14 years of my career continuously disappointed that this wasn't the case. And in 2013, I had had enough. I loved building products. I loved working with engineers. But I realized that, if I worked to change one startup at a time, I'd burn myself out. Instead, I took some time to reflect on how I could have a bigger impact, and I realized that companies fell into the trap of chasing the next sale or obsessing about their competitors because many companies (especially startups) didn't have a better model for product management. They didn't know what *good* looked like.

So I didn't just walk away from a job that day. I walked into my next career as a product-discovery coach. For the past seven years, I've been teaching product teams how to create successful products by obsessing about customer needs, pain points, and desires. I started with one-on-one product-manager coaching. I quickly learned that it wasn't enough to develop product managers, and my coaching evolved to teaching product managers, designers, and engineers how to make team decisions about what to build. With time, I came to view my coaching curriculum as a product in and of itself, and I started to measure the impact of how I coached. I tracked cohorts, I measured where teams got stuck, I iterated on my methods. Over time, my curriculum got better, and, as a result, the product teams that I worked with got better. Today, teams walk away from my 12-week coaching program equipped with an arsenal of continuous discovery habits that help them discover, iterate, and refine products that deliver value for their customers in a way that drives value for their businesses. My goal with this book is to share those habits with you in the hopes that you, too, will be inspired to spend more time with your customers. The world needs better products. It's up to us to make that happen. This book will teach you how.

PART I

WHAT IS CONTINUOUS DISCOVERY?

CHAPTER ONE

THE WHAT AND WHY OF CONTINUOUS DISCOVERY

How do you know that you are making a product or service that your customers want? How do you ensure that you are improving it over time? How do you guarantee that your team is creating value for your customers in a way that creates value for your business? In this book, you'll learn a structured and sustainable approach to continuous discovery that will help you answer each of these questions, giving you the confidence to act while also preparing you to be wrong. You'll learn to balance action with doubt, so that you can get started without being blindsided by what you don't get right.

Let's start at the beginning. All product teams do a set of activities to decide what to build and then do a different set of activities to build and deliver it. While you'll learn that these activities can and should overlap and interweave with each other, the work that is required to do each is fundamentally different. In this book, I'll refer to the work that you do to decide what to build as *discovery* and the work that you do to build and ship a product as *delivery*.[1] This distinction matters. As you'll see, many companies put a heavy

---

1   I first heard these terms used by Marty Cagan. See: https://svpg.com/
    the-origin-of-product-discovery/

emphasis on delivery—they focus on whether you shipped what you said you would on time and on budget—while under-investing in discovery, forgetting to assess if you built the right stuff. This book aims to correct for that imbalance.

Discovery isn't a one-time activity. A digital product is never done. It can and should continue to evolve. As we learn more about our market, as our customers' needs change, as new technology becomes available, good products adapt. This book will introduce a continuous discovery framework that enables teams to discover brand-new products and to iterate on existing ones. It will help you continuously discover unmet customer needs and the solutions that will address those needs. Before we get into how to do this, let's take a brief look at how we got here.

The Evolution of Modern Product Discovery

Product management is quickly evolving. Over the past 30 years, with the rise of the Internet, our industry has seen a rapid evolution in how we do both discovery and delivery. As a result, we see tremendous variation in our practice. Product management looks different everywhere. A brief history of the evolution of modern discovery can help us understand why this variation still exists. It can also give us a clear picture of how we can improve, wherever we are in the progression.

For many years, traditional discovery was not done by the product team. In the early days of software, business leaders owned discovery—they decided what to build. Discovery happened once a year in an annual budgeting process, where projects with fixed timelines were assigned to specific engineering teams. A project manager managed the work, budget, and schedule. Sometimes a product manager translated business needs to product requirements, but not always. There were (and still are) many challenges with this way of working. Software development is unpredictable.

Projects were often delivered late and over budget. Business needs often trumped customer needs. Teams learned after the product shipped that customers weren't excited about what they built. This way of working led to a lot of waste. Sadly, I still meet many teams and companies that work this way. Marty Cagan refers to these types of teams as delivery teams.[2]

Fortunately, in 2001, a group of engineers got fed up, went into the mountains, put their heads together, and came up with the Agile manifesto. This group of software engineers, influenced by the broader industry discussion about the pain points of developing software, proposed a number of principles to correct for what they saw. Projects were too big. Teams spent way too much time building the wrong stuff before they learned that customers didn't want it. The authors of the Agile manifesto advocated for shorter cycles with more frequent customer feedback. Second, they proposed working at a pace that could be sustained continuously, rather than furiously scurrying from one milestone to another. Third, they advocated for maximum flexibility—having the ability to adapt to customer feedback quickly and easily. And fourth, they advocated for simplicity. They were concerned with how much of what they built was never used or offered limited value and instead advocated for teams to ruthlessly limit what they built. You'll see these four principles infused throughout the methods in this book.

In the years following the Agile manifesto, teams worked to adopt these principles. We saw a rise in the adoption of Scrum and Kanban, two popular Agile frameworks, to manage delivery work. In parallel, we saw the growth of user-experience design and user research as means for collecting customer feedback. But this way of working also ran into challenges.

Leaders struggled to give up ownership of discovery. Even with shorter cycles and more customer feedback, business stakeholders still clung to their original ideas. Most teams weren't very good at

2   See https://svpg.com/product-vs-feature-teams/

estimating unpredictable work (who is?), and their shorter cycles, aptly named *sprints* in Scrum, truly became biweekly sprints, killing any chance of finding a continuously sustainable pace. The rest of the business continued operating on an annual budgeting cycle, making true flexibility nearly impossible. When teams learned something wouldn't work, they were still expected to deliver it on time and under budget. Usability testing was often done too late in the process, making it hard to address the substantial issues that were so often uncovered. User research was often outsourced to design agencies who did project-based research. And finally, teams continued to be measured by what they delivered, not whether anyone used it or if it created any value for the customer or the business.

However, it wasn't all bad news. Teams did shorten their delivery cycles. Companies iterated from annual releases to quarterly releases to monthly releases. Today, many teams work on a weekly or even daily release schedule. More frequent releases meant we could measure the impact of what we were building sooner. We got better at instrumenting our products. We got better at usability testing our solutions. We got better at starting small and iterating to bigger solutions. These were giant steps in the right direction. But we still struggled with deciding what to build. We still learned, after shipping code, that we'd built the wrong stuff.

More instrumentation, however, did make us acutely aware of this problem. We could now measure when we released a feature that nobody used, when we redesigned our navigation and our metrics didn't move, and when we added a product to our portfolio that nobody bought. These were hard lessons to learn. But the upside was that we started to question how we made decisions about what to build. We started with who should make those decisions. We started to push decision-making from business stakeholders to product managers and eventually to the whole product team. We started to question how we made discovery decisions. Instead of making them in conference rooms with just our own thoughts, we started engaging customers throughout the discovery process. Instead of just validating our ideas at the end of discovery, we started co-creating with customers from the very beginning. And our discovery cadence started to change. As our delivery cycles got shorter, so, too, did our discovery cycles. And this is where we are today.

Today, many teams are adopting, developing, and iterating on their own continuous discovery practices. They are engaging with customers on a regular basis. They are testing their assumptions. Rather than just validating their ideas, they are co-creating with customers—combining the team's knowledge of what's technically possible with the customer's knowledge of their own needs, pain points, and desires to build better products. They are doing all of this on a continuous cadence, supporting the continuous development of their products. They are adapting to changes in the market, in customer needs, and in technology, in real time. So can you. This book will show you how.

Who This Book Is For

Most successful digital products today are conceived, designed, built, and delivered by a cross-functional team composed of product managers, designers, and software engineers. Product managers bring the business context—they help teams ensure that the products they are building are viable for the business. They ensure that the business that supports the product will survive over time, allowing the team to further satisfy customers' needs. Designers bring visual, interactive, and systems-design chops that help to ensure that customers will understand how to best use a product and delight in that use. Software engineers bring the technical chops to ensure that the product is reliable, stable, and delivers on its promise. All three roles are critical to the success of any digital product. They are collectively responsible for ensuring that their products create value for the customer in a way that creates value for the business.

This book was written for **product people** (product managers, designers, and software engineers) who want to build products that their customers need and love. It outlines a collection of habits that, when deployed continuously week over week, lead to better business outcomes and better customer outcomes. These habits were designed to be adopted by a product trio composed of each of these roles. Throughout the book, the term "product trio" will refer to a product manager, a designer, and a software engineer working together to develop products for their customers.

A Product Trio

Now, most digital products require the input of more than three people. Most teams have several engineers contributing to the code base. Some teams have the luxury of having multiple designers or product managers contributing to the same product or unit of work. Additionally, most teams have other roles that contribute to the success of their product, including product marketers, data analysts, user researchers, and customer-success representatives, among others. Defining the product trio as I have done here is not meant to exclude any of these critical roles from the discovery process. Each team needs to define the right "trio" on their team to adopt these habits. I put *trio* in quotes because your trio might be a quartet or even a quintet.

As you read this book, if you choose to be more inclusive of who engages with these habits, just know that inclusion comes at a cost. The more folks involved in each decision, the longer it will take to reach that decision. You want to balance speed of decision-making with inclusiveness. For most teams, their trio needs to consist of at least a product manager, designer, and software engineer. For some teams it will make sense to add a fourth or even a fifth member to this decision-making squad. I trust you will use your best judgment to find what works best for your team.

And if you don't work in a product trio right now, don't worry— you can still adopt many of these habits today. But this book will encourage you to start thinking about how you can more closely collaborate with your cross-functional colleagues.

With your trio defined, let's turn to the mindsets you'll each need to develop in order to successfully adopt these continuous discovery habits.

The Prerequisite Mindsets

Many teams chase frameworks, tools, and methodologies, hoping that each new innovation will suddenly unlock the door to product success. However, for most frameworks, tools, and methodologies to be successful, it's not just your tactics that need to change but also your mindset. The same will be true for the tactics in this book. There are six mindsets that must be cultivated to successfully adopt the habits outlined in this book.

1. Outcome-oriented: The first mindset is both a mindset and a habit. You'll learn more about the habit in the coming chapters, but the mindset requires that you start thinking in outcomes rather than outputs. That means rather than defining your success by the code that you ship (your output), you define success as the value that code creates for your customers and for your business (the outcomes). Rather than measuring value in features and bells and whistles, we measure success in impact—the impact we have had on our customers' lives and the impact we have had on the sustainability and growth of our business.

2. Customer-centric: The second mindset places the customer at the center of our world. It requires that we not lose sight of the fact (even though many companies have) that the purpose of business is to create and serve a customer. We elevate customer needs to be on par with business needs and focus on creating customer value as well as business value.

3. Collaborative: The third mindset requires that you embrace the cross-functional nature of digital product work and reject the siloed model, where we hand off deliverables through stage gates. Rather than the product manager decides, the designer designs, and the engineer codes, we embrace a model where we make team decisions while leveraging the expertise and knowledge that we each bring to those decisions.

4. Visual: The fourth mindset encourages us to step beyond the comfort of spoken and written language and to tap into our immense power as spatial thinkers. The habits in this book will encourage you to draw, to externalize your thinking, and to map what you know. Cognitive psychologists have shown in study after study that human beings have an immense capacity for spatial reasoning.[3] The habits in this book will help you tap into that capacity.

5. Experimental: The fifth mindset encourages you to don your scientific-thinking hat. Many of us may not have scientific training, but, to do discovery well, we need to learn to think like scientists identifying assumptions and gathering evidence. The habits in this book will help you develop and hone an experimental mindset.

---

3   For a good summary of this research, see Barbara Tversky's *Mind in Motion*.

6. Continuous: And finally, these habits will help you evolve from a project mindset to a continuous mindset. Rather than thinking about discovery as something that we do at the beginning of a project, you will learn to infuse discovery continuously throughout your development process. This will ensure that you are always able to get fast answers to your discovery questions, helping to ensure that you are building something that your customers want and will enjoy.

A Working Definition of Continuous Discovery

In my experience working with product teams, many are already adopting many of the discovery activities you will learn about in this book. Customer interviews, usability testing, and A/B testing are pervasive. What is rare is for teams to adopt these discovery activities in a structured and sustainable way, enabling them to continuously infuse their product decisions with customer input. To distinguish teams who occasionally do modern discovery activities from teams who do continuous discovery, we'll adopt the following definition of continuous discovery:

> At a minimum, weekly touchpoints with customers
> By the team building the product
> Where they conduct small research activities
> In pursuit of a desired outcome

Product teams make decisions every day. Our goal with continuous discovery is to infuse those daily decisions with as much customer input as possible. If teams are only engaging with customers on a monthly basis, they are making a month's worth of decisions without customer input. Over the course of this book, you'll learn habits that will help you adopt a continuous cadence in a structured and sustainable way. You'll learn how to do your own research so that you can get fast answers to your daily questions. You'll learn how to modify traditional research activities to make them sustainable week over week. And most importantly, you'll learn to ensure that your research is in service of pursuing a desired business outcome while meeting customers' needs.

CHAPTER TWO

A COMMON FRAMEWORK FOR CONTINUOUS DISCOVERY

"Managers must convert society's needs into opportunities for profitable business."

— Peter Drucker

"If I had an hour to solve a problem, I'd spend 55 minutes thinking about the problem and 5 minutes thinking about solutions."

— Albert Einstein

2016 was a tough year for the American bank Wells Fargo. Several regulatory organizations uncovered fraudulent activity at the bank. Bankers were opening checking, savings, and credit-card accounts on behalf of customers without their customers' knowledge or prior approval. The news was picked up by newspapers across the country. It was a public-relations nightmare.

At first, Wells Fargo blamed individual branch employees, arguing the fraudulent activity was the result of isolated behavior. But under further scrutiny, it became clear that employees were under immense pressure from senior leadership to grow the average number of accounts held by each customer. For years, Wells Fargo was known for its cross-selling strategy, in which, once a customer opened one account with the firm, bankers would then work to grow that customer's footprint. If the customer opened a checking and savings account, bankers would offer a credit card or a mortgage.

With time, however, this cross-selling strategy became more and more aggressive. Bankers were given quotas that were impossible to reach. Because these quotas were paired with lucrative incentives, bankers looked for ways to cheat the system. Under immense pressure from senior leadership, tempted by the lure of compelling incentives, many bankers opened fraudulent accounts on their customers' behalf without their permission.

Wells Fargo was fined $185 million by the Consumer Financial Protection Bureau and faced lawsuits costing them billions of dollars as a result. The Wells Fargo story is a story of outcomes gone wrong. The company rightly started with a desired outcome: To increase the average number of accounts per customer. However, they didn't pair this outcome mindset with a customer-centric mindset, that is critical for long-term product success.[4]

While Wells Fargo's fraud is exceptional, the focus on outcomes at the cost of the customer is not uncommon. At many companies, there is a tension between business needs and customer needs. When you get bombarded with a handful of ads before you can start reading a newspaper article, it's because the newspaper prioritized their need for ad revenue over the reader's need for a pleasant reading experience. When you can't watch your favorite sporting event because the broadcast rights didn't allow it to be streamed in your region, the sports team prioritized their television revenue over their fans' desire to watch the game. When hotels tack on a resort fee that isn't visible at time of booking, the hotel is prioritizing their own short-term revenue needs over the traveler's

---

4 The details of this Wells Fargo story come from journalists' reports. I have not worked at or with Wells Fargo and have no direct knowledge of what happened. Here is one particularly detailed account: https://money.cnn.com/2018/04/24/news/companies/wells-fargo-timeline-shareholders/index.html

need for price transparency. Sadly, this conflict between business needs and customer needs is prevalent in every industry. But it doesn't have to be this way.

Businesses do need to make a profit. That's required for their survival. However, profit should not come at the cost of serving the customer. Renowned business consultant and author Peter Drucker, in the opening quote of this chapter, argues that the goal of a business is to "convert society's needs into opportunities for a profitable business." He argues that a company's purpose is to serve the customer. Instead of framing business needs as at odds with customer needs, Drucker is aligning the two, by arguing that serving customers is how we generate profit. I couldn't agree more. In this chapter, I'll introduce a framework for continuous discovery that will ensure that you pursue business needs by addressing your customers' needs.

Begin With the End in Mind

As our product-discovery methods evolve, we are shifting from an output mindset to an outcome mindset. Rather than obsessing about features (outputs), we are shifting our focus to the impact those features have on both our customers and our business (outcomes). Starting with outcomes, rather than outputs, is what lays the foundation for product success.

When a product trio is tasked with delivering an outcome, the business is clearly communicating what value the team can create for the business. And when the business leaves it up to the team to explore the best outputs that might drive that outcome, they are giving the team the latitude they need to create value for the customer. However, as we saw in the Wells Fargo story, we can't take customer value for granted.

When a product trio is tasked with an outcome, they have a choice. They can choose to engage with customers, do the work required to truly understand their customers' context, and focus on creating value for their customers. Or they can take short-cuts—they can focus on creating business value at the cost of customers. The organizational context in which the product trio works will have a big impact on which choice the product trio will make. Some teams, however, choose to take shortcuts because they simply don't know another way of working. The framework in this chapter and the habits described in this book will help you resolve the tension between business needs and customer needs so that you can create value for your customers *and* your business.

The Challenge of Driving Outcomes

Most product trios don't have a lot of experience with driving outcomes. They grew up in a world where they were told what to build. Or they were asked to generate outputs, with little thought for what impact those outputs had. So, when we shift from an output mindset to an outcome mindset, we have to relearn how to do our jobs.

Unfortunately, it's not as simple as talking to customers every week. That's a good start. But we also need to consider the rest of our continuous-discovery definition:

> At a minimum, weekly touchpoints with customers
> By the team building the product
> Where they conduct small research activities
> In pursuit of a desired outcome

I've met many teams who are good at talking to customers. But they forget that the purpose of these customer touchpoints is to conduct research in pursuit of a desired outcome. Those last two lines of the definition are critical. We aren't doing research for research's sake. We are doing research so that we can serve our customers in a way that creates value for our business.

Finding the best path to your desired outcome is what researchers call an "ill-structured problem"—also commonly called a "wicked problem." Ill-structured problems are defined by having many solutions. There are no right or wrong answers, only better or worse ones. Much of the work when tackling an ill-structured problem is framing the problem itself.[5] How we frame a problem has a big impact on how we might solve it. For example, in the Wells Fargo story, their leadership, whether implicitly or explicitly, had framed the problem as "grow customer accounts at all costs." This framing opened the door to cheating. If, on the other hand, Wells Fargo had framed the problem as "create customers who want to open more accounts," bankers would have been less likely to cheat.

If product trios tasked with delivering a desired outcome want to pursue business value by creating customer value, they'll need to work to frame the problem in a customer-centric way. They'll need to discover the customer needs, pain points, and desires that, if addressed, would drive their business outcome. For example, if Wells Fargo had learned what inspired customers to open new accounts, they might have found a customer-centric way to reach their outcome.

In this book, I'll refer to customer needs, pain points, and desires collectively as "opportunities"—they represent opportunities to intervene in our customers' lives in a positive way. Why don't we call them "problems to solve"? In the product world, we don't just solve customer problems. The word "problem" implies something needs fixing. However, we have many examples of products or services that don't fix problems. Disneyland entertains me. Ice cream is delicious. Mountain biking is fun. These products address my

---

5   Jonassen, D. H. (1997). Instructional design models for well-structured and ill-structured problem-solving learning outcomes. Educational Technology Research and Development, 45(1), 65–94.

desires. I could try to shoehorn these desires into needs—I need something to fill my time, I need nutrients, and I need exercise. However, writing a book, eating spinach, and going to the gym might be more effective ways of addressing those needs. The key difference here is that I enjoy Disneyland, ice cream, and mountain biking. These products were designed to address my desires, not solve my problems. So, to make sure this model is more inclusive of such products, I'll use opportunities to represent customer needs, pain points, and desires collectively and the *opportunity space* to represent the problem space as well as the desire space.

To reach their desired outcome, a product trio must discover and explore the opportunity space. The opportunity space, however, is infinite. This is precisely what makes reaching our desired outcome an ill-structured problem. How the team defines and structures the opportunity space is exactly how they give structure to the ill-structured problem of reaching their desired outcome. David Jonassen, an educational psychologist from the University of Missouri, studied ill-structured problem-solving and highlights the importance of problem *framing*. How we frame an ill-structured problem impacts how we might solve it. Additionally, Jonassen suggests that we can't simply start with one framing. Instead, he argues, good problem-solvers try out many framings, exploring how each impacts the solution space.[6]

The implication for product trios is that two of the most important steps for reaching our desired outcome are first, how we map out and structure the opportunity space, and second, how we select which opportunities to pursue. Unfortunately, many product trios skip these steps altogether. They start with an outcome and simply

6   Jonassen, D. H. (1997). Instructional design models for well-structured and ill-structured problem-solving learning outcomes. Educational Technology Research and Development, 45(1), 65–94.

start generating ideas. We do have to get to solutions—shipping code is how we ship value to our customers and create value for our business. But the right problem framing will help to ensure that we explore and ultimately ship better solutions.

The Underlying Structure of Discovery

Back in 2016, I was coaching a product trio who were learning to adopt a continuous cadence for the first time. One day they told me, "Teresa, we are learning a lot of discovery tactics, but we have no idea what to do when. You always tell us our next steps. How are we supposed to do this on our own?" This question floored me. The last thing I wanted was to create a dependency on me. But I didn't have an easy answer for them. How did I decide what to do next in discovery?

After some reflection[7], I realized there's an underlying structure to discovery that we can use to guide our work. It starts with defining a clear outcome—one that sets the scope for discovery. From there, we must discover and map out the opportunity space—this is what gives structure to the ill-structured problem of reaching our desired outcome. It's the all-important problem *framing* that opens up the solution space. And finally, we need to discover the solutions that will address those opportunities and thus drive our desired outcome.

It sounds simple, but this structure helps us know what to do when. I encourage teams to visualize it using an opportunity solution tree (OST).

---

7   I blogged about this experience at ProductTalk.org/ost-origin

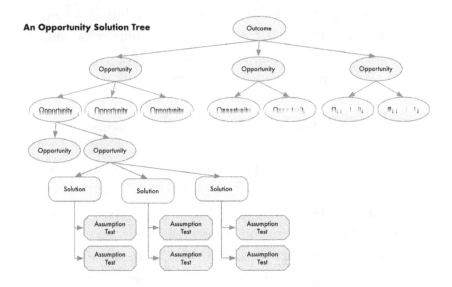

Opportunity solution trees are a simple way of visually representing the paths you might take to reach a desired outcome.

The root of the tree is your desired outcome—the business need that reflects how your team can create business value.

Next is the opportunity space. These are the customer needs, pain points, and desires that, if addressed, will drive your desired outcome.

Below the opportunity space is the solution space. This is where we'll visually depict the solutions we are exploring.

Below the solution space are assumption tests. This is how we'll evaluate which solutions will help us best create customer value in a way that drives business value.

Opportunity solution trees have a number of benefits. They help product trios:

- Resolve the tension between business needs and customer needs
- Build and maintain a shared understanding of how they might reach their desired outcome
- Adopt a continuous mindset

- Unlock better decision-making
- Unlock faster learning cycles
- Build confidence in knowing what to do next
- Unlock simpler stakeholder management

We'll explore each of these benefits throughout this chapter.

OSTs Resolve the Tension Between Business Needs and Customer Needs

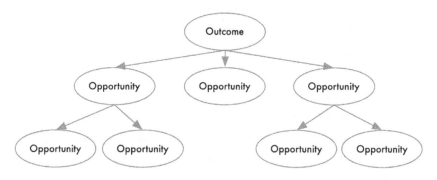

Only include opportunities that are relevant to your outcome

Opportunity solution trees help you resolve the tension between business needs and customer needs. You start by prioritizing your business need—creating value for your business is what ensures that your team can serve your customer over time. Next, the team should explore the customer needs, pain points, and desires that, if addressed, would drive that outcome. The key here is that the team is filtering the opportunity space by considering only the opportunities that have the potential to drive the business need. By mapping the opportunity space, the team is adopting a customer-centric framing for how they might reach their outcome.

The outcome and the opportunity space constrain the types of solutions the product trio might consider. This is what helps us avoid Wells Fargo's fate and sets us up to create value for our customers and our business.

OSTs Help Build and Maintain a Shared Understanding Across Your Trio

For most of us, when we encounter a problem, we simply want to solve it. This desire comes from a place of good intent. We like to help people. However, this instinct often gets us into trouble. We don't always remember to question the framing of the problem. We tend to fall in love with our first solution. We forget to ask, "How else might we solve this problem?"

These problems get compounded when working in teams. When we hear a problem, we each individually jump to a fast solution. When we disagree, we engage in fruitless opinion battles. These opinion battles encourage us to fall back on our organizational roles and claim decision authority (e.g., the product manager has the final say), instead of collaborating as a cross-functional team.

When a team takes the time to visualize their options, they build a shared understanding of how they might reach their desired outcome. If they maintain this visual as they learn week over week, they maintain that shared understanding, allowing them to collaborate over time. We know this collaboration is critical to product success.

OSTs Help Product Trios Adopt a Continuous Mindset

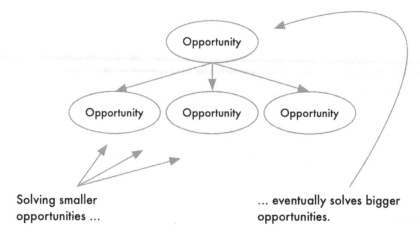

Solving smaller opportunities ...

... eventually solves bigger opportunities.

Shifting from a project mindset to a continuous mindset is hard. We tend to take our six-month-long waterfall project, carve it up into a series of two-week sprints, and call it "Agile." But this isn't Agile. Nor is it continuous. A continuous mindset requires that we deliver value every sprint. We create customer value by addressing unmet needs, resolving pain points, and satisfying desires.

The opportunity solution tree helps teams take large, project-sized opportunities and break them down into a series of smaller opportunities. As you work your way vertically down the tree, opportunities get smaller and smaller. Teams can then focus on solving one opportunity at a time. With time, as they address a series of smaller opportunities, these solutions start to address the bigger opportunity. The team learns to solve project-sized opportunities by solving smaller opportunities continuously.

OSTs Unlock Better Decision-Making

As product trios explore the best path to their desired outcome, they need to make key decisions along the way. It's easy to get lost. When you bounce from tactic to tactic, it's easy to forget what you've learned and what decisions you need to make next.

Chip and Dan Heath, in their book *Decisive*, outline four villains of decision-making that lead to poor decisions. The first villain is looking too narrowly at a problem. This is exactly why we want to explore multiple ways of framing the opportunity space. The second villain is looking for evidence that confirms our beliefs. This is commonly known as *confirmation bias*. We'll be discussing this bias often throughout the book. We'll be exploring several habits that will help us overcome this bias and ensure that we are considering both confirming and disconfirming evidence. The third villain is letting our short-term emotions affect our decisions. In the product world, this often shows up when we fall in love with our ideas. The fourth villain is overconfidence. This, too, is common in the product world. We are often sure our ideas will be runaway successes.

In *Decisive*, the Heath brothers outline many tactics for overcoming the four villains of decision-making, which is why it is the first book (after this one) that I recommend all product managers read. But the one tactic we'll rely on over and over again throughout this book is their advice to avoid "whether or not" decisions. A "whether or not" decision is when we frame a problem as "Should we do this or not?" Product trios get caught up in "whether or not" decisions when we react to one customer need or pain point at a time, asking, "Should we stop everything and fix this problem?" We also encounter "whether or not" decisions when a stakeholder asks us to implement their pet feature, and we ask, "Should we stop everything and build this feature?" This is perhaps the most common mistake product trios make.

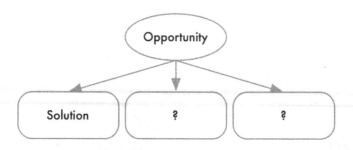

What else could we build?

Instead of framing our decisions as "whether or not" decisions, this book will teach you to develop a "compare and contrast" mindset. Instead of asking, "Should we solve this customer need?" we'll ask, "Which of these customer needs is most important for us to address right now?" We'll compare and contrast our options. Instead of falling in love with our first idea, we'll ask, "What else could we build?" or "How else might we address this opportunity?" Visualizing your options on an opportunity solution tree will help you catch when you are asking a "whether or not" question and will encourage you, instead, to shift to a compare-and-contrast question.

Even with this decision-making framework in hand, you'll still need to guard against overconfidence (the fourth villain of decision-making). It's easy to think that, when you've done discovery well, you *can't* fail, but that's simply not true (as we'll see in a few stories throughout this book). Good discovery doesn't prevent us from failing; it simply reduces the chance of failures. Failures will still happen. However, we can't be afraid of failure. Product trios need to move forward and act on what they know today, while also being prepared to be wrong. The habits in this book will help you balance *having confidence* in what you know with *doubting* what you know, so that you can take action while still recognizing when you are on a risky path.[8]

And finally, we can't talk about decision-making without tackling the dreaded problem of *analysis paralysis*. Many of the decisions we make in discovery feel like big strategic decisions. That's because they often are. Deciding what to build has a big impact on our company strategy, on our success as a product team, and on our customers' lives. However, most of the decisions that we make in discovery are reversible decisions. If we do the necessary work to test our decisions, we can quickly correct course when we find that we made the wrong decision. This gives us the luxury of moving quickly, rather than falling prey to analysis paralysis. The habits in this book will teach you how to make fast decisions and then quickly test to understand the consequences of those decisions. You'll learn to adapt as you go rather than slow down to analyze.

Visualizing each decision point and the options that you considered on the opportunity solution tree will help you revisit past decisions when needed and will give you the context you need to course-correct.

OSTs Unlock Faster Learning Cycles

Many organizations try to define clear boundaries between the roles in a product trio. As a result, some have come to believe that product managers own defining the *problem* and that designers and software engineers own defining the *solution*. This sounds nice in theory, but it quickly falls apart in practice.

---

8   Karl Weick, a psychologist at the University of Michigan, defines this balance of having confidence in what you know with doubting what you know as the "essence of wisdom." See: "Karl Weick. The Attitude of Wisdom: Ambivalence as the Optimal Compromise." Published in *Organizational Wisdom and Executive Courage*.

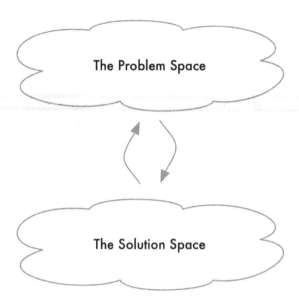

The problem space and the solution space evolve together.

Nigel Cross, Emeritus Professor of Design Studies at the Open University in the United Kingdom, compared the knowledge, skills, and abilities of expert designers to novice designers (across a variety of disciplines) and found that the best designers evolve the problem space and the solution space together.[9] As they explore potential solutions, they learn more about the problem, and, as they learn more about the problem, new solutions become possible. These two activities are intrinsically intertwined. The problem space and the solution space evolve together.

When we learn through testing that an idea won't work, it's not enough to move on to the next idea. We need to take time to reflect. We want to ask: "Based on my current understanding of my customer, I thought this solution would work. It didn't. What did I misunderstand about my customer?" We then need to revise our

9   Nigel Cross, "Expertise in design: an overview." *Design Studies*, Volume 25, Issue 5, 2004, 427–441, ISSN 0142-694X, https://doi.org/10.1016/j.destud .2004.06.002.

understanding of the opportunity space before moving on to new solutions.[10] When we do this, our next set of solutions get better. When we skip this step, we are simply guessing again, hoping that we'll strike gold.

All of the habits and methods in this book are designed to be completed together by the product trio. The last thing we want to do is use our organizational roles as an excuse to artificially sever the ties between the problem space and the solution space. The product trio should be responsible for both.

By visually mapping out the opportunity space on an opportunity solution tree, a product trio is making their understanding of their customer explicit. When a solution fails, they can revisit this mapping to quickly revise that understanding.

OSTs Build Confidence in Knowing What to Do Next

As a product trio gains experience with opportunity solution trees, the shape of their tree will help guide their discovery work. The depth and breadth of the opportunity space reflects the team's current understanding of their target customer. If our opportunity space is too shallow, it can guide us to do more customer interviews. A sprawling opportunity space, on the other hand, reminds us to narrow our focus. If we aren't considering enough solutions for our target opportunity, we can hold an ideation session. If we don't have enough assumption tests in flight, we can ramp up our testing.

While many teams work top-down, starting by defining a clear desired outcome, then mapping out the opportunity space, then considering solutions, and finally running assumption tests to

---

10   This isn't unique to design. John Dewey, an American educational philosopher, argues that this is the key to strong critical thinking. When we encounter something that surprises us (like a failed solution), we need to critically examine the beliefs that led to that surprise so that we can update them. If you want to learn more about Dewey's thoughts on critical thinking, see his book *How We Think*.

evaluate those solutions, the best teams also work bottom-up. They use their assumption tests to help them evaluate their solutions and evolve the opportunity space. As they learn more about the opportunity space, their understanding of how they might reach their outcome (and how to best measure that outcome) will evolve. These teams work continuously, evolving the entire tree at once.

They interview week over week, continuing to explore the opportunity space, even after they've selected a target opportunity. They consider multiple solutions for their target opportunity, setting up good "compare and contrast" decisions. They run assumption tests across their solution set, in parallel, so that they don't overcommit to less-than-optimal solutions. All along, they visualize their work on their opportunity solution tree, so that they can best assess what to do next.

OSTs Unlock Simpler Stakeholder Management

Organizational change happens unevenly. Even when a company tasks a team with a clear desired outcome, it can be hard for leaders to let go of dictating outputs. This is especially true during times of stress, when we tend to fall back on old habits. As a result, it's not enough for a product trio to make evidence-based decisions about what to build; they also need to justify those decisions to key stakeholders along the way.

Unfortunately, many teams struggle to get this right. When it comes to sharing work with stakeholders, product trios tend to make two common mistakes. First, they share too much information— entire interview recordings or pages and pages of notes without any synthesis—expecting stakeholders to do the discovery work with them. Or second, they share too little of what they are learning, only highlighting their conclusions, often cherry-picking the research that best supports those conclusions. In the first instance, we are asking our stakeholders to do too much, and, in the second, we aren't asking enough of them. The key to bringing stakeholders along is to show your work. You want to summarize what you are learning in a way that is easy to understand, that highlights your key decision points and the options that you considered, and creates space for them to give constructive feedback. A well-constructed opportunity solution tree does exactly this.

When sharing your discovery work with stakeholders, you can use your tree to first remind them of your desired outcome. Next, you can share what you've learned about your customer, by walking them through the opportunity space. The tree structure makes it easy to communicate the big picture while also diving into the details when needed. Your tree should visually show what solutions you are considering and what tests you are running to evaluate those solutions. Instead of communicating your conclusions (e.g., "We should build these solutions"), you are showing the thinking and learning that got you there. This allows your stakeholders to truly evaluate your work and to weigh in with information you may not have.

Building Out Your Opportunity Solution Tree

The habits in this book will help your trio build out and evolve an opportunity solution tree.

As you embark on the wandering paths of discovery, your tree will act as your roadmap, helping you find the best path to your desired outcome.

PART II

CONTINUOUS DISCOVERY HABITS

In this part, you'll get introduced to 11 habits that, collectively, will help you adopt a structured and sustainable approach to continuous discovery. You'll learn to:

- Shift from an output mindset to an outcome mindset (Chapter 3).
- Frame, refine, and prioritize the opportunity space (Chapters 4–7).
- Generate and evaluate targeted solutions (Chapters 8–10).
- Measure the impact of your work all the way through to delivery so that delivery fuels discovery (Chapter 11).
- Manage the messy cycles of discovery, keeping you on track, even when you learn something surprising (Chapter 12).
- Show your work, bringing your stakeholders along throughout the discovery process (Chapter 13).

CHAPTER THREE

FOCUSING ON OUTCOMES OVER OUTPUTS

*"An outcome is a change in human behavior
that drives business results."*
— Josh Seiden, *Outcomes Over Output*

*"Too often we have many competing goals
that all seem equally important."*
— Christina Wodtke, *Radical Focus*

Sonja Martin, a product manager at tails.com—a Direct to Consumer business offering tailor-made dog food via a subscription service—and her team were tasked with improving a core business outcome, customer retention. While tails.com had many happy subscribers, they found that customer retention during the first 90 days of service was a critical indicator of long-term retention. Sonja's team set out to improve retention measured at the 90-day mark. However, they quickly ran into challenges.

Even though they started with a clear outcome, Sonja's team struggled to measure the impact of their product changes. As her team experimented with how to improve short-term retention, they found they had to wait 90 days before they could evaluate the impact of their ideas. As a result, they revised their metric to 30-day retention in an attempt to speed up their experiment cycles. This was also too long. They wanted to experiment week over week. So again, they changed their metric to 5-day retention. However, they were concerned that 5-day retention might not be a leading indicator of 30-day, 90-day, or long-term retention. So, while it allowed them to experiment faster, they weren't sure if they were driving their business outcome.

During their customer interviews, Sonja's team uncovered two primary factors that led to customer churn. First, not all tails.com customers understood the value of tailor-made dog food, and, second, some dogs simply didn't like the food. Sonja's team realized that they could prevent churn, and thus increase retention, if they focused on increasing the perceived value of tailor-made dog food and if they increased the number of dogs that liked the food. Their customer interviews helped them identify two product outcomes that were more actionable—they could measure their impact on both metrics right away, and they believed if they drove both, they would, in turn, drive their business outcome of increasing retention.[11]

Sonja's story illustrates many of the challenges that arise when shifting to an outcome mindset. It's not as simple as choosing a metric and running with it. Teams tasked with a new outcome often have no idea how to measure that outcome, how to impact it, or even if it's the right outcome to be pursuing. Lagging indicators like 90-day retention make it hard to measure the impact of fast experiment cycles. Product teams often have to do some discovery work to identify the connections between product outcomes (the metrics they can influence) and business outcomes (the metrics that drive the business). This chapter will help you translate business outcomes into product outcomes you can deliver, negotiate appropriate product outcomes with your leadership team, and determine when to set learning goals versus performance goals.

---

11   To read more about Sonja Martin's story, see: https://www.producttalk.org/ 2020/08/actionable-outcomes/

Why Outcomes?

Business thought leaders have been advocating for managing by outcomes for decades. Peter Drucker, a renowned managerial thought leader, wrote about its benefits countless times[12]. Andy Grove, the former CEO of Intel, utilized the practice at Intel and wrote about it in his best-selling book *High Output Management.* More recently, Google, Google Ventures[13], and John Doerr[14], a venture capital partner at Kleiner Perkins, have popularized the topic again with their advocacy for objectives and key results (OKRs)[15], one flavor of managing by outcomes. You'll hear from prominent thought leaders in most industries and broadly across the technology sector (including from me) that shifting from dictating outputs to managing by outcomes is critical to a company's success.

When we manage by outcomes, we give our teams the autonomy, responsibility, and ownership to chart their own path. Instead of asking them to deliver a fixed roadmap full of features by a specific date in time, we are asking them to solve a customer problem or to address a business need. The key distinction with this strategy over traditional roadmaps is that we are giving the team the autonomy to find the best solution. If they are truly a continuous-discovery team, the product trio has a depth of customer and technology knowledge, giving them an advantage when it comes to making decisions about how to solve specific problems.

Additionally, this strategy leaves room for doubt. A fixed roadmap communicates false certainty. It says we know these are the right features to build, even though we know from experience

---

12   For a good overview of Peter Drucker's thoughts on managing by outcomes, see the book: *The Essential Drucker*

13   See: https://library.gv.com/how-google-sets-goals-okrs-a1f69b0b72c7

14   See his book *Measure What Matters* (but also see this blog post for some valid criticisms of this book: https://felipecastro.com/en/blog/book-review-measure-what-matters/)

15   For a better book on OKRs, see Christina Wodtke's *Radical Focus*

their impact will likely fall short. An outcome communicates uncertainty. It says, *We know we need this problem solved, but we don't know the best way to solve it.* It gives the product trio the latitude they need to explore and pivot when needed. If the product trio finds flaws with their initial solution, they can quickly shift to a new idea, often trying several before they ultimately find what will drive the desired outcome.

Finally, managing by outcomes communicates to the team how they should be measuring success. A clear outcome helps a team align around the work they should be prioritizing, it helps them choose the right customer opportunities to address, and it helps them measure the impact of their experiments. Without a clear outcome, discovery work can be never-ending, fruitless, and frustrating.

All of this sounds fantastic. Is managing by outcomes really as good as it sounds? This is a hard question to answer. Industry best practices are clear. The best teams are adopting an outcome-focused mindset. However, the research is limited and conflicting. In this chapter, we'll start with what we can learn from industry practice, and then we'll look at how the research either supports or refutes that practice.

Exploring Different Types of Outcomes

Managing by outcomes is only as effective as the outcomes themselves. If we choose the wrong outcomes, we'll still get the wrong results. When considering outcomes for specific teams, it helps to distinguish between business outcomes, product outcomes, and traction metrics. A business outcome measures how well the business is progressing. A product outcome measures how well the product is moving the business forward. A traction metric measures usage of a specific feature or workflow in the product.

Business Outcomes	Measure business value	Retention
Product Outcomes	Measure how the product drives business value	Dogs who like the food
Traction Metrics	Tracks usage of specific features	Owners who use the transition calendar

Business outcomes start with financial metrics (e.g., grow revenue, reduce costs), but they can also represent strategic initiatives (e.g., grow market share in a specific region, increase sales to a new customer segment). Many business outcomes, however, are lagging indicators. They measure something after it has happened. It's hard for lagging indicators to guide a team's work because it puts them in react mode, rather than empowers them to proactively drive results. For Sonja's team, 90-day retention was a lagging indicator of customer satisfaction with the service. By the time the team was able to measure the impact of their product changes, customers had already churned. Therefore, we want to identify leading indicators that predict the direction of the lagging indicator. Sonja's team believed that increasing the perceived value of tailor-made dog food and increasing the number of dogs who liked the food were leading indicators of customer retention. Assigning a team a leading indicator is always better than assigning a lagging indicator.

As a general rule, product trios will make more progress on a product outcome rather than a business outcome. Remember, product outcomes measure how well the product moves the business forward. By definition, a product outcome is within the product trio's span of control. Business outcomes, on the other hand, often require coordination across many business functions.

For example, suppose Sonja's team discovered that, in addition to some customers not understanding the value of tailor-made dog food and some dogs not liking the food, poor customer-support response times and surprise price increases that occurred after their trial period ended also influenced their high churn rate. In this case, product, marketing, and customer support might need to coordinate their efforts to increase retention.

Coordination isn't bad. In fact, most of the work that we do will require coordination across teams. However, we can increase the accountability of each team by assigning a metric that is relevant to their own work. In this example, we might ask the product team to increase the number of dogs who like the food (something within the product team's span of control), whereas we might ask the marketing team to increase the transparency of the pricing after the trial ends, and we might ask the customer-support team to decrease their average response times. All three groups are contributing to the business outcome of increasing customer retention, but each is doing so in the way that they can best contribute.

Assigning product outcomes to product trios increases a sense of responsibility and ownership. If a product team is assigned a business outcome, it's easy for the trio to blame the marketing or customer-support team for not hitting their goal. However, if they are assigned a product outcome, they alone are responsible for driving results. When multiple teams are assigned the same outcome, it's easy to shift blame for lack of progress.

Finally, when setting product outcomes, we want to make sure that we are giving the product trio enough latitude to explore. This is where the distinction between product outcomes and traction metrics can be helpful. It's also a key delineation between an outcome mindset and an output mindset. If Sonja's team believes more dogs would like the food if their owners had a better transition plan, why not get more specific with the outcome? For example, they could launch a transition calendar and measure engagement with that calendar as their outcome. This strategy, however, assumes that the transition calendar is the right output. If it's not—if it turns out that customers don't want to use the transition calendar—then Sonja's team is stuck. They don't have the latitude to explore alternative solutions. Even though it looks like they were focused on an outcome (engagement with the transition calendar), they were really fixated on an output (the transition calendar itself).

When we assign traction metrics to product trios, we run the risk of painting them into a corner by limiting the types of decisions that they can make. Product outcomes, generally, give product trios far more latitude to explore and will enable them to make the decisions they need to ultimately drive business outcomes. However, there are two instances in which it is appropriate to assign traction metrics to your team.

First, assign traction metrics to more junior product trios. Improving a traction metric is more of an optimization challenge than a wide-open discovery challenge and is a great way for a junior team to get some experience with discovery methods before giving them more responsibility. For your more mature teams, however, stick with product outcomes.

Second, if you have a mature product and you have a traction metric that you know is critical to your company's success, it makes sense to assign this traction metric to an optimization team. For example, Sonja's team may already know that customers want to use the transition calendar—perhaps they use it every day—but the recommended schedule isn't as effective as they hoped it would be. In this case, it might make sense to have a team focused on optimizing the schedule. If the broader discovery questions have already been answered, then it's perfectly fine to assign a traction metric to a team. The key is to use traction metrics only when you are optimizing a solution and not when the intent is to discover new solutions. In those instances, a product outcome is a better fit.

Outcomes Are the Result of a Two-Way Negotiation

Setting a team's outcome should be a two-way negotiation between the product leader (e.g., Chief Product Officer, Vice President of Product, etc,) and the product trio.

The product leader brings the across-the-business view of the organization to the conversation and should communicate what's most important for the business at this moment in time. But to be clear, the product leader should not be dictating solutions. Instead, the leader should be identifying an appropriate product outcome for the trio to focus on. Outcomes are a good way for the leader to communicate strategic intent. For example, if Sonja's team is focused on increasing the number of dogs who like the food, her product leader can encourage her to keep focusing on the number of dogs who like the food broadly. Or, based on the strategic needs of the business, the leader might refine this outcome to have the team focus on specific breeds or strategic geographic regions. The key is that the leader should not narrow the scope so much that the team is tasked with a traction metric—engagement with the transition calendar.

The product trio brings customer and technology knowledge to the conversation and should communicate how much the team can move the metric in the designated period of time (usually one calendar quarter). The trio should not be required to communicate what solutions they will build at this time, as this should emerge from discovery.

For example, Sonja's team, if asked to focus on a specific customer segment, might summarize what they know about that customer segment, share how successful past attempts to get dogs to like the food in that customer segment have been, and estimate how much impact they can have on the metric in the designated time period (e.g., we can increase the number of dogs in that segment who like the food by 10% in the next three months).

This then sets the stage for the two-way negotiation. If the business needs the team to have a bigger impact on the outcome, the trio will need to adjust their strategy to be more ambitious, and the product leader will need to understand that more ambitious outcomes carry more risk. The team will need to make bigger bets to increase their chance of success, but these bigger bets typically come with a higher chance of failure. Similarly, the product leader and product trio can negotiate resources (e.g., adding engineers to the team) and/or remove competing tasks from the team's backlog, giving them more time to focus on delivering their outcome.

A particular scenario of note is when teams are assigned an outcome for the first time—as we saw in Sonja's story. In these cases, the product trio will need some time to learn what might move the metric. This is why a stable product trio focused on the same outcome over time is so critical. Every time we mix up the team or change the outcome, we take a learning tax as the team gets up to speed.

Encouraging a two-way negotiation between the product leader and the product trio ensures that the right organizational knowledge is captured during the selection of the outcome. It, however, has another benefit. Bianca Green, business faculty at University of Twente (in the Netherlands), and her colleagues found that teams who participated in the setting of their own outcomes took more initiative and thus performed better than colleagues who were not involved in setting their outcomes[16]. This is an area where the research supports industry best practice.

---

16   See: Groen, B., Wilderom, C., & Wouters, M. (2017). "High Job Performance Through Co-Developing Performance Measures With Employees." *Human Resource Management,* 56(1), 111–132.

Do You Need S.M.A.R.T. Goals?

Common goal-setting advice encourages us to set specific, measurable, achievable, relevant, and time-bound (S.M.A.R.T.) goals. The research on goal setting, however, muddies the waters.

Researchers have found that teams that set specific, challenging goals outperform teams who don't. Challenging goals create focus, inspire effort and persistence, and help to surface relevant organizational knowledge. However, there are some caveats. The team has to believe that they can achieve the goal, and they need to be committed to the goal, further supporting the idea that teams need to be involved in defining their own outcomes. Teams also need continuous feedback on their progress toward their goal, supporting the argument that goals should be measurable.[17]

However, much of this goal-setting research was conducted using simple, straightforward tasks. More recent research on goal setting involving more complex tasks, like the ones product trios face, found that challenging goals can decrease performance if the team doesn't have strategies for how to achieve their goal. These studies found that encouraging teams to "do their best" was more effective than setting specific, challenging goals. Additionally, these studies found that setting an initial *learning* goal (e.g., discover the strategies that might work) was more effective than setting a *performance* goal. Only once appropriate strategies were identified

---

17   For a good summary of this research, see: Latham, GP, Locke, Edwin A, & Latham, Gary P. (2002). "Building a practically useful theory of goal setting and task motivation: A 35-year odyssey." *American Psychologist*, 57(9), 705–717.

did performance increase with a specific, challenging performance goal.[18]

This research suggests that product trios, when faced with a new outcome, should first start with a learning goal (e.g., discover the opportunities that will drive engagement) before being tasked with a performance goal (e.g., increase engagement by 10%). This approach can be particularly helpful because it's common to have uncertainty around the best way to measure your outcome. We often need to do some discovery to learn how to best measure a product outcome. For example, when Sonja's team started investigating retention as an outcome, they had no idea what they would uncover. Rather than spinning their wheels trying to define the perfect, specific, measurable retention metric, her team focused on learning what led to churn and used that knowledge to revise their metric over time.

S.M.A.R.T. goals play a role and are common for trios that have experience with their product outcomes. But it's not one-size-fits-all. It's perfectly fine to start with a learning goal and work your way toward a S.M.A.R.T. performance goal.

A Guide for Product Trios

Product trios tend to fall into four categories when it comes to setting outcomes: 1) they are asked to deliver outputs and don't work toward outcomes (this is, by far, the most common scenario); 2) their product leader sets their outcome with little input from the team; 3) the product trio sets their own outcomes with little input from their product leader; 4) the product trio is negotiating their outcomes with their leaders as described in this chapter.

18 For a summary of this research, see: Latham, GP, Tasa, K, Latham, BW, Seijts, G H, Latham, G P, & Latham, B W. (2004). "Goal Setting and Goal Orientation: An Integration of Two Different, Yet Related, Literatures." *The Academy of Management Journal*, 47(2), 227–239.

If you are being asked to deliver outputs with no regard for outcomes, try these tips to shift toward a more outcome-focused mindset:

- When your product leader assigns a new initiative to your product trio, ask your leader to share more of the business context with you. Explore these questions:
    - Who is the target customer for this initiative?
    - What business outcome are we trying to drive with this initiative?
    - Why do we think this initiative will drive that outcome? (Be careful with *Why?* questions. They can put some leaders on the defensive. Use your best judgment, based on your knowledge of your specific leader.)
- Try to connect the dots between the business outcome and potential product outcomes. Can you clearly define how this new initiative will impact a product outcome? Is that outcome a leading indicator of the lagging indicator, business outcome?

If your product leader is asking you to deliver an outcome with no input from your team, try these tips to shift to a two-way negotiation:

- If you are being asked to deliver a business outcome, try mapping out which product outcomes might drive that business outcome, and get feedback from your leader.
- If you are being asked to deliver a product outcome, ask your leader for more of the business context. Try asking, "What business outcomes are we trying to drive with this product outcome?"

- In either case, clearly communicate how far you think you can get in the allotted time.

If your team is setting their own outcome with no input from the product leader, try these tips to shift to a two-way negotiation:

- Before you set your own outcome, ask your product leader for more business context. Try these questions:
  - What's most important to the business right now? Try to frame this conversation in terms of business outcomes.
  - Is there a customer segment that is more important than other customer segments?
  - Are there strategic initiatives we should know about?
- Use the information you gain to map out the most important business outcomes and what product outcomes might drive those business outcomes. Get feedback from your leader.
- Choose a product outcome that your team has the most influence over.

If your product trio is already negotiating outcomes with your product leader, congratulations! However, remember to keep these tips in mind as you set outcomes with your leader:

- Is your team being tasked with a product outcome and not a business outcome or a traction metric?
- If you are being tasked with a traction metric, is the metric well known? Have you already confirmed that your customers want to exhibit the behavior being tracked?
- If it's the first time you are working on a new metric, are you starting with a *learning* goal (e.g., discover

the relevant opportunities) before committing to a challenging *performance* goal?

- If you have experience with the metric, have you set a specific and challenging goal?

Avoid These Common Anti-Patterns

When setting product outcomes, avoid these common anti-patterns. Anti-patterns are common patterns that should be avoided.

Pursuing too many outcomes at once. Most of us are overly optimistic about what we can achieve in a short period of time. No matter how hard we work, our companies will always ask more of us. Put these two together, and we often see product trios pursuing multiple outcomes at once. What happens when we do this is that we spread ourselves too thin. We make incremental progress (at best) on *some* of our outcomes but rarely have a big impact on *any* of our outcomes. Most teams will have more of an impact by focusing on one outcome at a time.

Ping-ponging from one outcome to another. Because many businesses have developed fire-fighting cultures—where every customer complaint is treated like a crisis—it's common for product trios to ping-pong from one outcome to the next, quarter to quarter. However, you've already learned that it takes time to learn how to impact a new outcome. When we ping-pong from outcome to outcome, we never reap the benefits of this learning curve. Instead, set an outcome for your team, and focus on it for a few quarters. You'll be amazed at how much impact you have in the second and third quarters after you've had some time to learn and explore.

Setting individual outcomes instead of product-trio outcomes. Because product managers, designers, and software engineers typically report up, to their respective departments, it's not uncommon for a product trio to get pulled in three different directions, with each member tasked with a different goal. Perhaps the product manager is tasked with a business outcome, the designer is tasked with a usability outcome, and the engineer is tasked with a technical-performance outcome. This is most common at companies that tie outcomes to compensation. However, it has a detrimental effect. The goal is for the product trio to collaborate to achieve product outcomes that drive business outcomes. This isn't possible if each member is focused on their own goal. Instead of setting individual outcomes, set team outcomes.

Choosing an output as an outcome. Shifting to an outcome mindset is harder than it looks. We spend most of our time talking about outputs. So, it's not surprising that we tend to confuse the two. Even when teams intend to choose an outcome, they often fall into the trap of selecting an output. I see teams set their outcome as "Launch an Android app" instead of "Increase mobile engagement" or "Get to feature parity on the new tech stack" instead of "Transition customer to the new tech stack." A good place to start is to make sure your outcome represents a number even if you aren't sure yet how to measure it. But even then, outputs can creep in. I worked with a team that helped students choose university courses who set their outcome as "Increase the number of course reviews on our platform." When I asked them what the impact of more reviews was, they answered, "More students would see courses with reviews." That's not necessarily true. The team could have increased the number of reviews on their platform, but if they all clustered around a small number of courses, or if they were all on courses that students didn't view, they wouldn't have an impact. A better outcome is "Increase the number of course views that include reviews." To shift your outcome from less of an output to more of an outcome, question the impact it will have.

Focusing on one outcome to the detriment of all else. Like we saw in the Wells Fargo story, focusing on one metric at the cost of all else can quickly derail a team and company. In addition to your primary outcome, a team needs to monitor health metrics to ensure they aren't causing detrimental effects elsewhere. For example, customer-acquisition goals are often paired with customer-satisfaction metrics to ensure that we aren't acquiring unhappy customers. To be clear, this doesn't mean one team is focused on both acquisition and satisfaction at the same time. It means their goal is to increase acquisition without negatively impacting satisfaction.

DISCOVERING OPPORTUNITIES

The next four habits will help you discover, structure, and prioritize the opportunity space. You'll get introduced to three key artifacts that will help you build a shared understanding as you work to discover the best path to your desired outcome.

- You'll start by building an experience map that reflects what you currently know about your customer (Chapter 4).
- Your experience map will guide you as you interview customers to discover specific opportunities. You'll capture what you are learning from each interview on an interview snapshot (Chapter 5).
- You'll map out and structure those opportunities on an opportunity solution tree (Chapter 6) and use the tree structure to help you assess and prioritize the opportunity space (Chapter 7).

These artifacts are not intended to be one-time activities. Instead, they'll continue to evolve as your understanding of your customer's context (your experience map) and their needs, pain points, and desires (the opportunity space on your opportunity solution tree) evolve.

CHAPTER FOUR

VISUALIZING WHAT YOU KNOW

*"Whether actual or virtual, an external
representation creates common ground..."*
— Barbara Tversky, *Mind in Motion*

*"If we give each other time to explain ourselves using
words and pictures, we build shared understanding."*
— Jeff Patton, *User Story Mapping*

I coached a newly formed product trio who was tasked with an
outcome for the first time. Their product required a long application process that some customers neglected to complete. This
team's outcome was to increase the rate of application submissions. Each member of the trio had their own idea about what
was preventing customers from submitting their application. And
each person brought a unique set of knowledge and experiences
to the trio. The product manager had been with the company for
a couple of years but was new to the product-manager role. The
designer was the company's new Vice President of Design and
joined a trio to get an on-the-ground view of how the company
worked. The engineer had the longest tenure at the company but
had little discovery experience.

In the previous chapter, you learned that, to chart the best path to a desired outcome, you need to discover and map out the opportunity space. However, the opportunity space is infinite. You can't just dive in. You'll quickly get lost. To make sense of the opportunity space, we first need to take an inventory of what we already know. This is especially critical on cross-functional teams, where each member brings a diverse set of knowledge and experiences.

When working with an outcome for the first time, it can feel overwhelming to know where to start. It helps to first map out your customers' experience as it exists today. This trio started by mapping out what they thought was preventing their customers from submitting their applications. But they didn't do so by getting together in a room to discuss what they knew. Instead, they started out with each product-trio member mapping out their own perspective. This was uncomfortable at first. The designer had little context for what might be going wrong. The engineer had a lot of technical knowledge but had little firsthand contact with customers. The product manager had some hunches as to what was going wrong but didn't have any analytics to confirm those hunches. They each did the best they could.

Once they had each created their individual map, they took the time to explore each other's perspectives. The product manager had the best grasp of the "known" challenges—the customer complaints that made their way to their call center and through support tickets. The designer missed a few steps in the process but did a great job of capturing the confusion and insecurity that the customer might be feeling in the process. Because he was new to the company, he was able to view the application process from an outsider's perspective. The engineer's map accurately captured the process and added detail about how one step informed another step. This uncovered insights into how a customer might get derailed if an earlier step had been completed incorrectly.

Each map represented a unique perspective—together they represented a much richer understanding of the opportunity space they intended to explore. The trio quickly worked to merge their unique perspectives into a shared experience map that better reflected what they collectively knew. Their map wasn't set in stone. They knew that it contained hunches and possibilities, not truth. But it gave them a clear starting point. They had made explicit what they thought they knew, where they had open questions, and what they needed to vet in their upcoming customer interviews.

This chapter will teach you how to use your desired outcome as a starting point to work your way—first individually, and then as a team—to an experience map that reflects what you know about your customers' experience today. You'll learn to visualize your own perspective, explore the perspectives of your teammates, and then use the myriad of perspectives to co-create a shared team understanding. This shared map will guide your customer interviews, and it will help give structure to the opportunity space. It can and should evolve week over week as your team learns about your customers.

Set the Scope of Your Experience Map

To get started, you'll want to first set the scope of your experience map. If you start jotting down everything you know about your customer, you'll quickly get overwhelmed. Instead, start with your desired outcome. The trio in the opening story was trying to increase application submissions, so they mapped out what they thought their customers' experience was as they filled out the application. They specifically focused on this question: "What's preventing our customers from completing their application today?" Their outcome constrained what they tried to capture.

Think strategically about how broad or narrow to set the scope. When a team is focused on an optimization outcome, like increasing application submissions, it's fine to define the scope narrowly. However, when working on a more open-ended outcome, you'll want to expand the scope of your experience map.

For example, if we worked at a streaming-entertainment company (e.g., Netflix, Hulu) and we were tasked with an outcome like "increase the average minutes watched," we might set our scope broadly: "How do customers entertain themselves today?" With this scope, we might capture everything we know about how customers choose, engage with, and consume streaming entertainment. But given the scope of the question, we might also capture what we know about their behavior when socializing with friends, attending sporting events and concerts, reading books, and playing video games. This might be the right scope, if we are looking to explore adjacent markets. But for most teams, this scope is too broad.

However, we don't want to define our scope too narrowly, either. If we define our scope as "How do customers entertain themselves using our service?" we rule out any inspiration we might get from how they use other streaming-entertainment services, how they entertain themselves through their cable or satellite-dish packages, or how they entertain themselves through services like Twitch and YouTube. If, however, we define our scope as "How do customers entertain themselves with video?" we constrain the scope, but not too much.

Now you could easily argue that the scope should be "How do customers entertain themselves with video, music, and video games?" Or even, "How do customers entertain themselves online?" These options could all work. There's not one right scope. The key is to have a conversation as a team about the scope that gives you room to explore while staying focused on your outcome. Once you've defined the scope of your experience map, you are ready to take an inventory of your individual knowledge before working to develop a shared understanding of what you collectively know.

Start Individually to Avoid Groupthink

It's easy when working in a team to experience groupthink. Groupthink occurs when a group of individuals underperform due to the dynamics of the group. There are a number of reasons for this. When working in a group, it's common for some members to put in more effort than others; some group members may hesitate or even refrain from speaking up, and groups tend to perform at the level of the least-capable member.[19] In order to leverage the knowledge and expertise in our trios, we need to actively work to counter groupthink.

To prevent groupthink, it's critical that each member of the trio start by developing their own perspective before the trio works together to develop a shared perspective. This is counterintuitive. It's going to feel inefficient. We are used to dividing and conquering, not duplicating work. But in instances where it's important that we explore multiple perspectives, the easiest way to get there is for each product-trio member to do the work individually.

Experience Maps Are Visual, Not Verbal

Many of us stopped drawing sometime in elementary school. As a result, we have the drawing skills of a child. This makes drawing uncomfortable. Regardless of how well you draw, drawing is a critical thinking aid that you will want to tap into. Drawing allows us to externalize our thinking, which, in turn, helps us examine that thinking. When we draw an experience map, rather than verbalize it, it's easier to see gaps in our thinking, to catch what's missing, and to correct what's not quite right.[20]

---

19   You can learn more about groupthink in Leigh Thompson's *Making the Team: A Guide for Managers*

20   If you are interested in learning more about the cognitive benefits of drawing, check out cognitive psychologist Barbara Tversky's book *Mind in Motion*.

If you are feeling intimidated by the idea of drawing an experience map, don't worry. You don't need to draw well. You can draw boxes and arrows, stick figures, and squiggly shapes that mean something only to you. The goal is not to create a piece of art but rather to visualize your thinking so that you can examine it.

Start with the scope of your experience map. Our product trio that opened the chapter started with the question, "What's preventing our customers from completing the application today?" In our streaming-entertainment example, we might start with the question, "How do consumers entertain themselves with video?"

When thinking about this question, don't focus on your product. Instead, draw the experience of your customer. For example, our product trio didn't draw a screen-by-screen wireflow of their application process. Instead, they drew the process as their customers perceived it. They captured where they got stuck, what went wrong, how they course-corrected, and where they eventually abandoned the process.

In our streaming-entertainment example, we don't want to draw a screen-by-screen flow of how to use Netflix. Instead, we want to think about the broader context. When and where does video play a role in a user's life? How do they hear about content? How do they make decisions about what to do when? Who do they do it with? What challenges and obstacles do they face along the way?

The following is a simple experience map that might address the question, "How do customers entertain themselves with videos?" It starts with how someone might hear about content, who they share it with, the need to search for it, the challenges that might arise from trying to find it, the viewing experience, and, ultimately, success. As we learn about our customers, we'll add far more detail to the map, including the myriad of ways people hear about content, the different services they might have to bounce between, the different devices they watch on, and so much more.

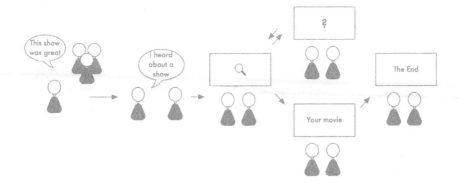

As you get started, you are going to be tempted to describe this context with words. Don't. Language is vague. It's easy for two people to *think* they are in agreement over the course of a conversation, but, still, each might walk away with a different perspective. Drawing is more specific. It forces you to be concrete. You can't draw something specific if you haven't taken the time to get clear on what those specifics are. Your goal during this exercise is to do the work to understand what you know, not to generalize vague thoughts about your customer. So set aside some time, grab a pen and paper, and start drawing. Push through the discomfort of being a beginner, and you'll be reaping the benefits in no time.

Once each member of your trio has taken the time to inventory what they know, it's time to explore the diverse perspectives on your team.

Explore the Diverse Perspectives on Your Team

Take turns sharing your drawings among your trio. As you explore your teammates' perspectives, ask questions to make sure you fully understand their point of view. Give them time and space to clarify what they think and why they think it. Don't worry about what they got right or wrong (from your perspective). Instead, pay particular attention to the differences. Be curious.

When it's your turn to share, don't advocate for your drawing. Simply share your point of view, answer questions, and clarify your thinking.

Remember, everyone's perspective can and should contribute to the team's shared understanding. We saw in our opening story that the trio's shared map was stronger because they synthesized the unique perspectives on the team into a richer experience map than any of them could have individually created.

Once you have a clear understanding of each team member's perspective, you are ready to start building a shared team perspective.

Co-Create a Shared Experience Map

As you work together to co-create a shared experience map, focus on synthesizing your work together rather than choosing the "best" drawing to move forward with.

Start by turning each of your individual maps into a collection of nodes and links. A node is a distinct moment in time, an action, or an event, while links are what connect nodes together. For example, my map of how customers entertain themselves might include the following nodes: hearing about a new show, discussing it with their significant other, a searching or browsing moment, the error case of not being able to find the content, the time spent being entertained, and the end of the entertainment session. Links help show relationships between the nodes. For example, I might loop back several times in this process. Perhaps I choose Netflix but can't find anything to watch, so I switch to YouTube. Links can show the movement through the nodes.

Create a new map that includes all of your individual nodes. Arrange the nodes from all of your individual maps into a new, comprehensive map.

Collapse similar nodes together. Many of your individual maps will include overlapping nodes. Feel free to collapse similar nodes together. However, be careful. Make sure you are collapsing like items and not generalizing so much that you lose key detail.

Determine the links between each node. Use arrows to show the flow through the nodes. Don't just map out the happy path. Remember to capture where steps need to be redone, where people might give up out of frustration, or where steps might loop back on themselves.

Add context. Once you have a map that represents the nodes and links of your customer's journey, add context to each step. What are they thinking, feeling, and doing at each step of the journey? Try to capture this context visually. It will help the team (and your stakeholders) synthesize what you know, and it will be easier to build on this shared understanding.

Avoid Common Anti-Patterns

As you work to visualize what you know, avoid these common anti-patterns.

Getting bogged down in endless debate. If you find yourself debating minute details, try to draw out your differences instead of debating them. We often debate details when we already agree. We just don't realize we already agree. When you are forced to draw an idea, you have to get specific enough to define what it is. This often helps to quickly clear up the disagreement or to pinpoint exactly where the disagreement occurs. Drawing really is a magic tool in your toolbox. Use it often.

Using words instead of visuals. Because many of us are uncomfortable with our drawing skills, we tend to revert back to words and sentences. Instead, use boxes and arrows. Remember, you don't have to create a piece of art. Stick figures and smiley faces are perfectly okay. But drawing engages a different part of your brain than language does. It helps us see patterns that are hard to detect in words and sentences. When I was first learning to draw, I was reluctant. I still don't draw well, but I now draw every day. The more you draw, the more you'll realize drawing is a superpower.

Moving forward as if your map is true. One of the drawbacks of documenting a customer-experience map is that it can start to feel like truth. Remember, this is your first draft, intended to capture what you think you know about your customer. We'll test this understanding in our customer interviews and again when we start to explore solutions.

Forgetting to refine and evolve your map as you learn more. It can be easy to think of this activity as a one-time event. However, as you discover more about your customer, you'll want to make sure that you continue to hone and refine this map as a team. Otherwise, you'll find that your individual perspectives will quickly start to diverge even when you are working with the same set of source data. Each person will take away different points from the same customer interview or the same assumption test. You'll want to continuously synthesize what you collectively know so that you maintain a shared understanding of your customer context.

CHAPTER FIVE
CONTINUOUS INTERVIEWING

Some people say, "Give the customers what they want." But
that's not my approach. Our job is to figure out what they're
going to want before they do. I think Henry Ford once said, "If
I'd asked customers what they wanted, they would have told
me, 'A faster horse!'" People don't know what they want until
you show it to them. That's why I never rely on market research.
Our task is to read things that are not yet on the page.
— Steve Jobs, CEO of Apple, in Walter Isaacson's *Steve Jobs*

"Confidence is a feeling, which reflects the coherence of the
information and the cognitive ease of processing it. It is wise to
take admissions of uncertainty seriously, but declarations of high
confidence mainly tell you that an individual has constructed a
coherent story in his mind, not necessarily that the story is true."
— Daniel Kahneman, *Thinking, Fast and Slow*

Steve Jobs, the founder and former CEO of Apple, often dis-
counted market research. He argued, "People don't know what
they want until you show it to them." Jobs was right. Customers
don't always know what they want. Most aren't well-versed in
technology. Nor do they have time to dream up what's possible.
That's our job. That's what Jobs meant when he said, "Our task is

to read things that are not yet on the page." We are the inventors, not our customers.

However, this doesn't mean we shouldn't be talking to our customers. In this chapter, you will learn why interviewing on a regular cadence is critical to the success of any product trio and how to build a habit of interviewing weekly.

The purpose of customer interviewing is not to ask your customers what you should build. Instead, the purpose of an interview is to discover and explore opportunities. Remember, opportunities are customer needs, pain points, and desires. They are opportunities to intervene in your customers' lives in a positive way.

Steve Jobs knew the importance of discovering opportunities better than most. He and the rest of the Apple team were masters at uncovering unmet needs. When the first iPhone was released in 2007, it wasn't the first smartphone on the market. People resisted the idea of an on-screen keyboard. There were no third-party apps. But even though Apple wasn't first to the market and they launched with a limited feature set, the first iPhone solved several customer needs that other smartphones didn't.

If you are too young to remember the first iPhone, one of the big features at release was visual voicemail. Visual voicemail is so familiar today, it's hard to remember what voicemail used to be like. Here's how *Ars Technica* described visual voicemail in their 2007 review:

> *Instead of requiring the user to dial up the carrier's voicemail number and listen to his or her voicemails in the order that they were received, visual voicemail lists each message out in visual format on the iPhone, almost like e-mail. It displays who the voicemail is from (and if it doesn't recognize the number, it will analyze the area code and tell you what geographical area it's from, which is helpful), and the user can tap whichever*

*one in the list that he or she wants, no matter its position
in the list. When the voicemail is playing, the user can
pause it, scrub back and forth in the message, or skip.*[21]

Now, if you had interviewed customers before the original
iPhone was released, nobody would have asked for visual voicemail. Nobody knew visual voicemail was possible. Most people
weren't even aware of their own pain points and challenges with
how regular voicemail worked. Voicemail wasn't important enough
for us to give it any thought.

Voicemail, at the time, was a minor inconvenience. To gain
access to your voicemail, you dialed your own phone number,
entered a password, and listened to each message sequentially.
One by one, you had to decide if you wanted to replay a message,
keep it, or delete it. If you had five messages and you needed to
hear the third message, you had to decide what to do with the first
two messages before you could get to the third one.

Voicemail was tedious. We were so accustomed to the tedium that
we no longer noticed it. In fact, voicemail was a vast improvement
over an earlier technology—tape-recorded answering machines.
Early answering machines required that you be at home to check
your messages. If you wanted to skip a message, you had to man-
ually fast-forward and hope that you stopped in the right spot to
hear the next message.

Voicemail, on the other hand, allowed you to check your messages from anywhere. You could quickly skip from one message
to the next. Jobs and his team, however, weren't satisfied. While
voicemail was better than early answering machines, it still presented pain points and challenges for the end-user. Apple uncovered
these opportunities and addressed them. Visual voicemail delighted
consumers.

---

21   See https://arstechnica.com/gadgets/2007/07/iphone-review/10/#h4

Apple is secretive about the way they work, so it's not clear if they interviewed users, observed friends and family, or simply identified these opportunities based on their own experience. But what is clear is that Apple is better than most at discovering opportunities.

For the rest of us, this chapter will cover how to use continuous interviewing to reliably find customer opportunities. As we saw with visual voicemail, we can't always rely on our customers to tell us what they need or want. Instead, you'll learn how to use your customers' own stories to discover their unmet needs.

The Challenges With Asking People What They Need

During a workshop, I asked a woman what factors she considered when buying a new pair of jeans. She didn't hesitate to answer. She said, "Fit is my number-one factor." I then asked her to tell me about the last time she bought a pair of jeans. She said, "I bought them on Amazon." I asked, "How did you know they would fit?" She replied, "I didn't, but they were a brand I liked, and they were on sale."

What's the difference between her two responses? Her first response tells me how she *thinks* she buys a pair of jeans. Her second response tells me how she *actually* bought a pair of jeans. This is a crucial difference. She thinks she buys a pair of jeans based on fit, but brand loyalty, the convenience of online shopping, and price (or getting a good deal) were more important when it came time to make a purchase.

This story isn't unique. I've asked people these same two questions countless times in workshops. The purchasing factors often vary, but there is always a gap between the first answer and the second. These participants aren't lying. We just aren't very good at understanding our own behavior.

Decades of research on investigative interviewing (the kind used by journalists, lawyers, and detectives) has shown that interview participants struggle to answer direct (factual) questions accurately.[22] In a witness interview, this might mean that the participant mistakes the color of the getaway car or forgets an important location. In a customer interview, this might mean that the customer misremembers when they bought something or forgets why they signed up for a particular service.

Direct questions require that we recall facts without context. This process is prone to cognitive biases—common patterns in mental errors that result from the way our brains process information.[23] We are bad at quantifying how often we do something. We often speculate about what we did, when, and why. We tend to favor generalities over specifics. We give answers that are influenced more by our sense of identity rather than our actual behavior. And we tend to come up with coherent reasons to explain our behavior that are often not grounded in reality. To be clear, this behavior is a function of how our brains work and not the result of interview participants trying to deceive us. In fact, many of these biases come into play because our interview subjects are trying to be helpful.

We see these errors show up in many contexts. Physically active adults overestimate how often they work out. Countless Americans underestimate how much alcohol they drink. The

---

22   To learn more:
- *Memory-Enhancing Techniques for Investigative Interviewing: The Cognitive Interview* Ronald Fisher, R.E. Geiselman—Charles C. Thomas Pub. Ltd., 1992
- *Evidence-Based Investigative Interviewing: Applying Cognitive Principles* Jason J. Dickinson, Nadja Schreiber Compo, Rolando N. Carol, Bennett L. Schwartz, Michelle R. McCauley—Routledge, 2019
- Brandon, S. E., Wells, S., and Seale, C. (2018). "Science-based interviewing: Information elicitation." *Journal of Investigative Psychology and Offender Profiling,* 15(2), 133–148. https://doi-org.turing.library.northwestern.edu/10.1002/jip.1496

23   For an in-depth summary of common cognitive biases, see Daniel Kahneman's *Thinking, Fast and Slow*

majority of us think we are above-average drivers, healthy eaters, and great listeners. It gets worse. Like the woman buying jeans, we think we understand why we do the things we do. But the reality is, our brains are exceptionally good at creating coherent (but not necessarily true) stories that deceive us.

Michael Gazzaniga, a neuropsychologist at the University of California Santa Barbara, conducted a phenomenal study that shows just how effective our brains are at deceiving us.[24] He constructed an experiment protocol in which split-brain patients were shown an image such that it was visible to only their left eye and asked the participant to select a related card with their left hand. Left-eye vision and left-side body movement are controlled by the right hemisphere. In a split-brain patient, the connection between the right and left hemispheres has been severed, meaning no information can cross from one hemisphere to the other. Therefore, in this protocol, the right hemisphere was doing all of the work, and the left hemisphere was unaware of what was happening.

Gazzaniga then asked participants why they chose the card that they did. Because language is processed and generated in the left hemisphere, the left hemisphere is required to respond. However, because of the protocol design, only the right hemisphere knows why the participant selected the card. As a result, Gazzaniga expected the participants to be stumped. But that isn't what happened. Instead, every subject fabricated a response.

The left hemisphere was being asked to provide a rationalization for a behavior done by the right hemisphere. The left hemisphere didn't know the answer. But that didn't keep the left hemisphere from fabricating an answer. That answer, however, had no basis in reality.

Now if this study had been limited to split-brain patients, it would be interesting but not very relevant to us. It turns out split-brain patients aren't the only ones who fabricate reasons. We all

24   See: *The Integrated Mind* Michael Gazzaniga, Joseph Ledoux—Plenum, 1981

do it. Gazzaniga named this tendency to rationalize our behavior even when we can't possibly know the reason as the "left brain interpreter," and later studies have shown that we all have an active "left brain interpreter."[25] We need to reconcile the present with the past, and when information is missing, our brains simply fill in details that make the story coherent.

This is exactly why in *Thinking, Fast and Slow*, behavioral economist Daniel Kahneman claimed, "A remarkable aspect of your mental life is that you are rarely stumped." Your brain will gladly give you an answer. That answer, however, may not be grounded in reality. In fact, Kahneman outlines dozens of ways our brains get it wrong. It's also why Kahneman argues confidence isn't a good indicator of truth or reality. He writes, "Confidence is a feeling, which reflects the coherence of the information and the cognitive ease of processing it." Not necessarily the truth.

As long as your brain can summon a compelling reason, it will feel like the truth—even if it isn't. Gazzaniga's participants thought they knew why they selected the card that they did. The left-brain interpreter filled in the missing details, creating a coherent story. The participant was confident—and, unfortunately, wrong.

Gazzaniga's study means you can't simply ask your customers about their behavior and expect to get an accurate answer. Most will obligingly give you what sounds like a reasonable answer. But you won't know if they are telling you about their *ideal* behavior or their *actual* behavior. Nor will you know if they are simply telling you a coherent story that sounds true but isn't true in practice.

I learned this the hard way. Back in 2007, I worked on a product that helped corporate recruiters source candidates. At that time, the hype in the recruiting industry was around recruiting passive candidates—candidates who were currently employed

25 *The Cognitive Neuroscience of Mind: A Tribute to Michael S. Gazzaniga*
    Patricia A. Reuter-Lorenz, Kathleen Baynes, George R. Mangun, and Elizabeth
    A. Phelps; The MIT Press; 2010; ISBN 0-262-01401-7

but open to new opportunities. There was a belief (and probably still is today) that passive candidates were better than active candidates—those who were unemployed and ready to apply for jobs right now. Thought leaders in the recruiting space advocated for recruiting passive candidates. Every customer I talked to told me they wanted to source passive candidates. I thought we had uncovered a real need. So, we built a passive-candidate-recruiting solution. It flopped.

Corporate recruiters said they wanted to source passive candidates. It's what their ideal selves wanted. It's what they aspired to. But when it came time to fill an open position, they sourced active candidates again and again. Why did this happen? Because recruiters are often measured by how fast they can fill an open role, and active candidates are the fastest way to do that. Even though recruiters aspired to source passive candidates, what they actually did was source active candidates. It's the equivalent of opening a salad bar across from a McDonald's because customers said they wanted to eat healthier. We can't be too surprised when our salads lose out to the Big Mac.

Our failure wasn't due to a lack of research. It was because we asked our customers the wrong questions. We built a product based on a coherent story told by both the thought leaders in our space and by our customers themselves. But it wasn't a story that was based in reality. If you want to build a successful product, you need to understand your customers' actual behavior—their reality—not the story they tell themselves.

Too often in customer interviews, we ask direct questions. We ask, "What criteria do you use when purchasing a pair of jeans?" Or we ask, "How often do you go to the gym?" But these types of questions invoke our ideal selves, and they encourage our brains to generate coherent but not necessarily reliable responses. In the coming pages, you'll learn a far more reliable method for learning about your customers' actual behavior.

Distinguish Research Questions From Interview Questions

The key to interviewing well is to distinguish what you are trying to learn (your research questions) from what you ask in the interview (your interview questions). Most product teams could generate an infinite list of research questions. There is always more to learn about our customers. We see some teams solve this by generating multi-page discussion guides. But this strategy assumes that you'll be talking to customers only occasionally, therefore, you need to ask them everything right now. Instead, assume you'll talk to customers every week, and focus on what you need to learn at this moment in time.

In any given interview, you'll want to balance broadly exploring the needs, pain points, and desires that matter most to that particular customer and diving deep on the specific opportunities that are most relevant to you. Every customer is unique, and, no matter how well you recruit, you may find that your customer doesn't care about the opportunity you most need to learn about. We don't want to spend time exploring a specific opportunity with a customer if that opportunity isn't important to them. Our primary research question in any interview should be: *What needs, pain points, and desires matter most to this customer?*

Once we've explored the opportunities that matter most to the customer, we can dive into the specifics of any of those opportunities. You may have specific opportunities in mind, but you'll want to let your participant set the direction of the interview. Remember, what matters most to your customer trumps what you need to learn.

Since we can't ask our customers direct questions about their behavior, the best way to learn about their needs, pain points, and desires is to ask them to share specific stories about their experience. You'll need to translate your research questions into interview questions that elicit these stories. Memories about recent instances are more reliable than our generalizations about our own behavior or our answers to direct questions.

Instead of asking, "What criteria do you use when purchasing a pair of jeans?"—a direct question that encourages our participant to speculate about their behavior—we want to ask, "Tell me about the last time you purchased a pair of jeans." The story will help us uncover what criteria our participant used when purchasing a pair of jeans, but because the answer is situated in a specific instance (an actual time when they bought jeans), it will reflect their actual behavior, not their perceived behavior.

Finding the right story question can be challenging. The scope of the story that you'll want to elicit will change throughout your discovery process. For example, if you work at a streaming-entertainment company and you are trying to increase viewer engagement, you might ask, "Tell me about the last time you watched our streaming-entertainment service." This question will help you learn about pain points and challenges with your product.

But you may want to widen the scope. You might say, "Tell me about the last time you watched any streaming entertainment." This question will elicit stories about your product but also stories about your competitors. You could broaden the scope even further to, "Tell me about the last time you were entertained." This might elicit stories about going to a movie theater, attending a concert, socializing with friends, and much more. This type of question is a great way to uncover what your product category (e.g., streaming entertainment) competes with.

You'll want to tailor the scope of the question based on what you need to learn at that moment in time. A narrow scope will help you optimize your existing product. Broader questions will help you uncover new opportunities. The broadest questions might help you uncover new markets. The appropriate scope will depend on the scope you set when creating your experience map (see Chapter 4).

Excavate the Story

As the interviewer, you will have to work to excavate the story. If you ask a participant to tell you about the last time they watched streaming entertainment, they will likely respond with something along the lines of: "I watched *The Good Place* last night after dinner." That's not a very good story.

Conversational norms set the expectation for a 50/50 back-and-forth pattern when two people are conversing. This means that each person spends roughly 50% of the time talking. I say something, and then you say something. If I ask you a short question, you are likely to respond with a short answer. As the interviewer, you need to reset this expectation. One of the most effective ways to do this is to inform your participant that you would like them to share their full story with you, to share as many details as possible, to leave nothing out, and that, when they are done with their story, you'll ask for missing details.

Even so, you may still have to dig to uncover the full story. You can use common storytelling tactics to help you do so. A good story has a protagonist who encounters experiences on a timeline. Temporal prompts are one of the most effective ways to guide the participant through their own story. You can ask, "Start at the beginning. What happened first?" You can use the experience map you created in Chapter 4 to help guide your participant. Prompt for the beginning of the story. If your participant isn't sure where to start, you can further prompt, "Where were you? Set the scene for me." As the participant tells their story, you can encourage them to keep going by asking them, "What happened next?" Sometimes they might skip a few steps, and you may need to ask, "What happened before that?" Thinking about their story as having a beginning, a middle, and an end can help you guide the participant. Use your customer-experience map to help you track their story. Listen for specific nodes. Ask about nodes that were left out of the story.

Stories also take place in specific locations; protagonists encounter challenges, and they receive help from supporting characters. Other characters might present obstacles or interfere with the protagonist's progress. Keep these elements in mind as they'll help you tease out what the participant forgets. You might ask, "Who was with you?" "What challenges did you encounter?" "How did you overcome that challenge?" "Did anyone help you?"

You'll notice, as you excavate the story, that your participant will bounce back and forth between the story they are telling and generalizing about their behavior. You might ask, "What challenges did you face?" and they may respond with, "I usually…" or, "In general, I have this challenge…" You'll want to gently guide them back to telling you about this specific instance. You might say, "In this specific example, did you face that challenge?"

Excavating the story takes practice. It might feel awkward at first. It will definitely feel inefficient. When your participant jumps to a generalization (e.g., "I always face this challenge"), it's going to feel like a shortcut. It's going to tempt you to conclude that's the real need, pain point, or desire. In those moments, it's critical that you remember the research on how poorly we perform at answering direct questions and how susceptible our responses are to cognitive biases.

Keep the interview grounded in specific stories to ensure that you collect data about your participants' actual behavior, not their perceived behavior. And remember, like most of the habits in this book, it takes practice. Don't get discouraged. Keep at it. You will get better with time.

You Won't Always Get What You Want

With story-based interviewing, you won't always collect the story that you want. That's okay. The golden rule of interviewing is to let the participant talk about what they care about most. You can steer the conversation in two ways.

First, you decide which type of story to collect. You can ask a more open question like: "Tell me about the last time you watched streaming entertainment." Or you can ask for a more specific story: "Tell me about the last time you watched streaming entertainment on a mobile device."

Second, you can use your story prompts to dig deeper into different parts of the story. If you are primarily concerned with how they chose what to watch, dig into that part of the story. If you aren't particularly interested in what device they watch on, don't ask for that detail if they leave it out of their story. Let your research questions guide your story prompts.

However, even so, you might encounter some participants who simply don't cooperate. They might not have a relevant story. They might be motivated to tell you about a different part of the story. They might not want to tell you a story at all. They might give one-sentence answers. Or they might want to share their feature ideas or gripe about how your product works.

In these instances, you'll want to do the best you can to capture the value the participant is willing to share, but don't force it. You always want to respect what the participant cares about most. Remember, with continuous interviewing, you'll be interviewing another customer soon enough. When we rarely interview, a disappointing interview can feel painful. When we interview continuously, a disappointing interview is easily forgotten.

Synthesize as You Go

When you continuously interview customers, there's no clear point at which to stop and synthesize what you are learning. Instead, you'll need to synthesize as you go. Meet the interview snapshot.

An interview snapshot is a one-pager designed to help you synthesize what you learned in a single interview. It's how you are going to turn your copious notes into actionable insights. Your collection of snapshots will act as a reference or index to the customer knowledge bank you are building through continuous interviewing.

After you've conducted even a handful of interviews, let alone the dozens you will conduct each year, interviews will start to blur together. You don't want to rely on your memory to keep your research straight. That's the job of an interview snapshot. Snapshots are designed to help you remember specific stories. They help you identify opportunities and insights from each and every interview.

The cliché "A picture is worth a thousand words" is true. The more visual your snapshot, the easier it will be for the team to remember the stories you collected—even weeks or months later. With permission, include a photo of the participant. Grab one from a social-media profile. Grab a screenshot from a video call. Snap a photo during an in-person interview. If your corporate guidelines require that you anonymize your interview data, or if you are interviewing participants about sensitive topics, skip the photo, and replace it with a visual that will help you remember their specific story. This could be a workplace logo, the car they drive, or even a cat meme that represents their story. The photo should help you put that interview snapshot into context. It should help you remember the stories that you heard.

At the top of the snapshot, include a quote that represents a memorable moment from their story. This might be an emotional quote or a distinct behavior that stood out. Like the photo, the quote acts as a key for unlocking your memory of the specific stories that they told. I can still remember memorable quotes from interviews that I did years ago. A couple of my favorites are "I've worked here for three years. But they feel like dog years." And "I'm old school. Agile doesn't work for me." When a participant uses vivid language, be sure to capture their exact words.

To help put a specific interview into context, you'll want to capture some quick facts about the customer. The quick facts will change from company to company, but they should help you identify what type of customer you were talking to. For example, a service that matches job candidates with companies might segment their employer customers by size (e.g., SMB, enterprise) or they might list average annual contract size. A streaming-entertainment service might list the customer's sign-up date and average hours watched each week. If they segment further, they might even include behavioral traits like binge-watcher or active referrer. The goal of the quick-facts section is to help you understand how the stories you heard in this interview may be similar to or different from those you heard from other customers.

The photo and the memorable quote will act as keys that help you to unlock your memory of the stories you heard. The quick facts help you situate those stories in the right context. Now you want to capture the heart of what you learned. You'll do this by identifying the insights and opportunities that you heard in the interview.

An opportunity represents a need, a pain point, or a desire that was expressed during the interview. Be sure to represent opportunities as needs and not solutions. If the participant requests a specific feature or solution, ask about why they need that, and capture the opportunity (rather than the solution). A good way to do this is to ask, "If you had that feature, what would that do for you?" For example, if an interviewee says, "I wish I could just *say* the name of the movie I'm searching for," that's a feature request. If you ask, "What would that do for you?" they might respond, "I don't want to have to type out a long movie title." That's the underlying need. The benefit of capturing the need and not just the solution is that the need opens up more of the solution space. We could add voice search to address this need, but we also could auto-complete movie titles as they type.

Opportunities don't need to be exact quotes, but you should frame them using your customer's words. This will help ensure that you are capturing the opportunity from your customer's perspective and not from your company's perspective.

Throughout the interview, you might hear interesting insights that don't represent needs, pain points, or desires. Perhaps the participant shares some unique behavior that you want to capture, but you aren't sure yet what to do with this information. Capture these insights on your interview snapshot. Over time, insights often turn into opportunities.

The goal with the snapshot is to capture as much of what you heard in each interview as possible. It's easy to discount a behavior as unique to a particular participant, but you should still capture what you heard on the interview snapshot. Be as thorough as possible. You'll be surprised how often an opportunity that seems unique to one customer becomes a common pattern heard in several interviews.

Draw the Stories You Collect

The experience map that you created in Chapter 4 will help guide each interview. As you collect each customer's unique story, you'll want to actively listen for how their story is similar to or different from your generalized experience map.

One of the most important elements to capture on the interview snapshot is an experience map that captures each participant's unique story. When creating an interview snapshot, our goal is to process and understand what we heard and to capture it in a way that will make our research referenceable and actionable in the future. These stories give us the knowledge we need to design for the right person, in the right context, at the right time. But it can only do that if we capture enough of the story to remember it when we need it.

Drawing the underlying structure of the stories that you hear—and, by that, I mean the nodes and the links that make up the story—will help you remember the story. It will help you better understand the story. We'll also see in the next chapter that drawing stories will help you find patterns across seemingly unique stories, which will be critical for making your body of research actionable. Drawing is a superpower that will help you unlock valuable insights from each interview.

Just as you saw in Chapter 4, drawing helps your team align around a shared understanding. Taking the time to capture visually what you learned from each interview will help you stay aligned as you learn more about your customers.

Interview Every Week

Weekly interviewing is foundational to a strong discovery prac-tice. Interviewing helps us explore an ever-evolving opportunity space. Customer needs change. New products disrupt markets.

Competitors change the landscape. As our products and services evolve, new needs, pain points, and desires arise. A digital product is never done, and the opportunity space is never finite or complete.

If interviewing is about discovering opportunities, it's easy to think that, once you've chosen a target opportunity, you can pause interviewing. But this assumes that you chose the *right* target opportunity, that you'll be able to address that opportunity, and that everything will go according to plan. If you need to change course and you've stopped interviewing, you'll have to start from scratch. Your next steps will be delayed until you can ramp up interviewing again. We don't want to think about interviewing as a step in a linear process. Instead, our goal is to interview continuously.

Raya Raycheva, a senior user researcher at Simply Business, an insurance company based in London, England, highlights the value of continuous interviewing:

> *"We recently had to pivot from one opportunity to another when we learned that the need we were exploring wasn't that important to our customers. Fortunately, because we were continuously interviewing, we didn't have to start from scratch. We could revisit our opportunity solution tree, choose a new opportunity, and start learning about it in our next set of interviews. We killed an opportunity on Tuesday, chose a new one on Wednesday, and used our already-scheduled interviews on Thursday to learn about the new opportunity."*

From a habit standpoint, it's much easier to maintain a habit than to start and stop a habit. If you interview every week, you'll be more likely to keep interviewing every week. Every week that you don't interview increases the chances that you'll stop interviewing altogether. To nurture your interviewing habit, interview at least one customer every week.

Automate the Recruiting Process

The hardest part about continuous interviews is finding people to talk to. In order to make continuous interviewing sustainable, we need to automate the recruiting process. Your goal is to wake up Monday morning with a weekly interview scheduled without you having to do anything.

Some teams have no problem recruiting interview participants, and they skip over this step. However, every team has weeks in which something goes wrong—a release goes awry, a significant prospect is at risk, a key team member is unexpectedly sick. It's during these weeks (that happen far more often than we like to admit) that you'll want to fall back on your recruitment automation to help you sustain your weekly interviewing habit.

When a customer interview is automatically added to your calendar each week, it becomes easier to interview than not to interview. This is your goal.

Recruit Participants While They Are Using Your Product or Service

The most common and easiest way to find interview participants is to recruit them while they are using your product or service. You can integrate a single question into the flow of your product: "Do you have 20 minutes to talk with us about your experience in exchange for $20?" Be sure to customize the copy to reflect the ask-and-offer that works best for your audience. If the visitor answers "Yes," ask for their phone number.

This strategy works best for high-traffic sites, where you can turn the survey on for a few minutes and get a response right away. If you don't have a high-traffic service, it may take hours or even days to get your first response. In this case, instead of asking for a phone number, ask the visitor to schedule an interview. Use scheduling software to reduce the back-and-forth required to find an available time.

For new products or services with few or no customers, you can still implement this strategy. Instead of recruiting people while they use your product (as it may not exist yet), you can use ads to drive traffic to a landing page. You can recruit people directly from the landing page.

Ask Your Customer-Facing Colleagues to Recruit

Most companies have teams who are on the phone with customers day in and day out. This includes sales teams, account managers, customer-success teams, and customer-support teams.

You can work with these teams to help you recruit interview participants. The easiest place to start is to ask a customer-facing colleague if you can join one of their existing meetings. Start by asking for five minutes at the end of a call. You want to make it as easy as possible for both your colleague and your customer to say "Yes." Use the last few minutes of an existing call to collect a specific story about the customer.

Once your customer-facing teams are comfortable with you joining their meetings, ask your customer-facing colleagues to help you schedule an interview with one of their customers. To make this work, you'll want to define triggers to help your customer-facing colleagues identify who to reach out to. Triggers might include:

- If a customer calls to cancel their subscription, schedule an interview.
- If a customer has a question about feature x, schedule an interview.
- If a customer requests a customization, schedule an interview.

Triggers can change week over week. The key is to clearly communicate to your customer-facing team who you would like to interview and to make it easy for them to schedule the interview. Give them a script to follow. It might be as simple as this: If the customer trigger occurs, then say: "I'd love for you to share your feedback with our product team. Can we schedule 20 minutes for you to talk with them?" If they say "Yes," have your colleague schedule the interview.

Interview Your Customer Advisory Board

If your customers are particularly hard to reach (e.g., doctors, CEOs), or if you have a small market (e.g., Canadian business schools, movie studios), the recruiting strategies we've covered will be challenging. Your customer's time is either too valuable, or you'll have concerns about reaching out to the same customers over and over again.

While most product teams worry their customers are too busy to talk with them, for most teams, this won't be true. We dramatically underestimate how much our customers want to help. If you are solving a real need and your product plays an important role in your customers' lives, they will be eager to help make it better. However, there are some audiences that are extremely hard to reach. In these instances, setting up a customer-advisory board will help.

Most companies use their customer-advisory boards to host focus groups. That may be valuable, but it's not a replacement for interviews. You can also use your customer-advisory board as interview participants. Invite your advisory-board members to participate in a monthly one-on-one interview. Offer an ongoing incentive as a reward for their participation.

You can scale the size of your customer-advisory board to reflect the number of interviews that your product teams need each month. If you have three product teams that each want to do one interview per week, you would invite 12 customers to participate on your advisory board.

One advantage of interviewing the same customers month over month is that you get to learn about their context in-depth and see how it changes over time. The risk is that you'll design your product for a small subset of customers that might not reflect the broader market. You can pair this recruiting method with one or two of the other methods to avoid this fate.

Interview Together, Act Together

Product trios should interview together. Some teams prefer to let one role, usually the product manager or the designer, be the "voice of the customer." However, our goal as a product trio is to collaborate in a way that leverages everyone's expertise. If one person is the "voice of the customer," that role will trump every other role.

Imagine that a product manager and a designer disagree on how to proceed. The designer has done all the interviewing. It's easy for the designer to argue, "This is what the customer wants." Whether or not that is true, the product manager has no response to that. Designating one person as the "voice of the customer" gives that person too much power in a team decision-making model. The goal is for *all* team members to be the voice of the customer.

Additionally, the more diverse your interviewing team, the more value you will get from each interview. What we hear in an interview will be influenced by our prior knowledge and experience.[26] A product manager will hear things that an engineer might not pick up on, and vice versa.

---

26 See Chris Argyris's model, "The Ladder of Inference," for why this is.

What does this look like in practice? Imagine you are interviewing a Netflix customer, and they tell you the following story:

> *Last night my wife and I, as we were finishing up dinner, decided we wanted to watch a movie. We wanted to watch on our big TV in the living room—it has better sound than the den—but our son was playing video games, so we had to wait for him to get to a good save point before he could switch to the den. As we waited, we scrolled through Netflix's movie selection on our iPad to figure out what we wanted to watch. Most of our recommendations were for kids' movies because it's mostly our kids who use the account. We tried "Most popular," but it was all TV shows. My wife remembered hearing about a good movie, but we couldn't figure out how to search for a specific movie title. It was very frustrating.*

The product manager might key in on, "'Most popular' was all TV shows" because they've been concerned that we don't have the right content. The designer might hear, "We couldn't figure out how to search for a specific movie title" because they are primarily interested in improving the user experience. The engineer might hear, "Most of the recommendations were for kids' movies" because they might be interested in finding a technical way to detect different types of users. All three selected different data as salient because of the perspectives they brought to the interview.

Each perspective is valid and can lead to an important product improvement. The more diversity in the room, the more value you'll get from each interview. And remember, an interview can be as short as five minutes. Everyone has time to spend a few minutes each week with a customer.

Avoid These Common Anti-Patterns

As you start building your continuous-interviewing habit, avoid these common anti-patterns.

Relying on one person to recruit and interview participants. If someone on your team takes the lead on recruiting and interviewing participants, it's easy to let them keep doing it. However, you want to avoid this. What happens when that person goes on vacation or is out sick unexpectedly? You don't want to have to skip or, even worse, cancel an interview because someone else on your team can't fill the gap. To make sure continuous interviewing is a robust habit, make sure everyone on your team is well-versed in recruiting and interviewing.

Asking who, what, why, how, and when questions. Long discussion guides exist for a reason. They are easy to create, and they allow everyone to get their favorite questions answered. Unfortunately, they lead to overwhelmed interview participants and unreliable interview data. Ditch the discussion guide. Instead, generate a list of research questions (what you need to learn), and identify one or two story-based interview questions (what you'll ask). Remember, a story-based interview question starts with, "Tell me about a specific time when..."

Interviewing only when you think you need it. It's easy to think discovery is a linear process. If we interview to identify customer opportunities, why can't we stop interviewing once we've chosen a target opportunity? Remember, it's much easier to continue a weekly habit than to start and stop a periodic behavior. Continuous interviewing ensures that you stay close to your customers. More importantly, continuous interviewing will help to ensure that you can get fast answers to your daily questions.

Sharing what you learned by sending out pages of notes and/ or sharing a recording. A product trio should share what they are learning with the rest of their team, their product peers, and with key stakeholders. However, when we share pages of notes that make sense only to us and/or a video of the full interview, we are expecting our colleagues to put as much effort into our discovery work as we do. This isn't feasible. They have their own jobs to do. Instead, use your interview snapshots to share what you are learning with the rest of the organization.

Stopping to synthesize a set of interviews. If you are used to a project world, you probably conduct 6 to 12 interviews and then stop to synthesize what you are learning. This usually involves stickies on a whiteboard, maybe some affinity diagramming, and ends in a research report that synthesizes what you learned. This, however, assumes that your interviews had a start and a stop. In a continuous-interviewing world, we don't start and stop. Instead, we interview every week. Rather than synthesizing a batch of interviews, synthesize as you go, using interview snapshots. The next chapter will also help you structure what you are learning to make it more actionable.

CHAPTER SIX

MAPPING THE OPPORTUNITY SPACE

"To maintain the state of doubt and to carry on systematic and protracted inquiry—these are the essentials of thinking."
— John Dewey, *How We Think*

"Structure is complicated. It gets done, undone, and redone."
— Barbara Tversky, *Mind in Motion*

Ahmed Guijou, a product director at Seera Group, had his world turned upside down overnight. He wasn't the only one. It was March 2020, and the COVID-19 pandemic had exploded around the world. Countries instituted stay-at-home orders, businesses shuttered, and travel ground to a halt. Before the pandemic, Guijou's team was on a mission to help "customers book their dream vacation or their business-trip accommodations in the easiest way possible." Once the pandemic hit, Saudi Arabia, home to most of Seera Group's customers, closed its borders, and Guijou's team saw their hotel-bookings business drop off overnight.

However, it wasn't all bad news. They noticed that some of their customers started looking for alternative accommodations closer to home. Instead of booking hotels and apartments in foreign countries, their customers were starting to book *Istrahas. Istraha*

97

means "resting place" in Arabic and generally refers to a large property with an outdoor area, barbecue, and a pool. Guijou's team, in previous customer interviews, had already uncovered that these properties were often used as day rentals to host social gatherings near home. While customers were no longer booking hotel accommodations, demand for *Istrahas* grew. Customers were looking for a safe place to connect with friends and family in the midst of a pandemic.

If Guijou and his team were to react to this shift in customer behavior, they had a lot to learn and little time to do so. Their marketplace had little *Istraha* inventory, and the team needed to figure out how to entice hosts to share their properties and how to get guests to consider their platform as the place to book. Guijou's team turned to their continuous discovery habits to guide them. They started interviewing *Istraha* hosts and guests. They uncovered countless opportunities on both sides of the marketplace. Rather than getting overwhelmed, they started mapping out the needs of each group on respective opportunity solution trees. They spent a few weeks collecting and sorting opportunities until patterns started to emerge. Guijou's team started grouping similar opportunities together. They paid particular attention to the needs, pain points, and desires that were specific to *Istraha* rentals. With each interview, the structure of the opportunity space continued to evolve.

When they felt they had a good understanding of the opportunity space, they took a step back to assess where they were. They looked for overlap between what hosts and guests each needed. They considered what their competition did well and where they saw gaps where they could compete. They started to see how they could leverage their existing strengths to play in this space.

By mapping out the opportunity space, Guijou's team was able to quickly assess where they could have an impact. In a few short weeks, they went from watching their business get disrupted overnight to identifying a new market opportunity and developing a product strategy for how they could tap into it.[27] That's the power of opportunity mapping.

The Power of Opportunity Mapping

As you collect customers' stories, you are going to hear about countless needs, pain points, and desires. Our customers' stories are rife with gaps between what they expect and how the world works. Each gap represents an opportunity to serve your customer. However, it's easy to get overwhelmed and not know where to start. Even if you worked tirelessly in addressing opportunity after opportunity for the rest of your career, you would never fully satisfy your customers' desires. This is why digital products are never complete. How do we decide which opportunities are more important than others? How do we know which should be addressed now and which can be pushed to tomorrow? It's hard to answer either of these questions if we don't first take an inventory of the opportunity space.

A single customer story might elicit dozens of opportunities. If you interview continuously, your opportunity space will always be evolving—expanding as you learn about new needs, contracting as you address known problems, and gaining clarity as you learn more about specific pain points. Mapping the opportunity space is a critical activity. Finding the best path to your desired outcome is an *ill-structured problem* (introduced in Chapter 2) and requires that we first structure or frame the problem space before we can dive into solving it. Mapping the opportunity space is how we give structure to the ill-structured problem of reaching our desired outcome.

It's easy, however, to bounce from one opportunity to the next, reacting to every need or pain point we hear about. Most product

27 To learn more about Ahmed Guijou and his team's story, see: https://www .producttalk.org/2020/12/discover-a-new-market/

teams are devoted to serving their customers, and, when they hear about a need or a pain point, they want to solve it. But our job is not to address every customer opportunity. Our job is to address customer opportunities that drive our desired outcome. This is how we create value for our business while creating value for our customers. Limiting our work to only the opportunities that might drive our desired outcome is what ensures that our products are viable over the long run and not just desirable in the moment.

Our goal should be to address the customer opportunities that will have the biggest impact on our outcome first. To do this, we need to start by taking an inventory of the possibilities. In the first quote that opens this chapter, John Dewey, an American educational philosopher, encourages us to "carry on systematic and protracted inquiry." Rather than jumping to the first need that we might address, Dewey argues, good thinking requires that we explore our options—that we carry out a systematic search for longer than we feel comfortable. We should compare and contrast the impact of addressing one opportunity against the impact of addressing another opportunity. We want to be deliberate and systematic in our search for the highest-impact opportunity.

In the second quote that opens this chapter, cognitive psychologist Barbara Tversky reminds us that structure "gets done, undone, and redone." As the opportunity space grows and evolves, we'll have to give structure to it again and again. As we continue to learn from our customers, we'll reframe known opportunities to better match what we are hearing. As we better understand how our customers think about their world, we'll move opportunities from one branch of the tree to another. We'll rephrase opportunities that aren't specific enough. We'll group similar opportunities together. These tasks will require rigorous critical thinking, but the effort will help to ensure that we are always addressing the most impactful opportunity.

In this chapter, you'll learn how to take an inventory of the opportunities that you are hearing in your interviews, and you'll learn how to give structure to the opportunity space in a way that ensures that you are always marching toward your desired outcome.

Taming Opportunity Backlogs

Some teams are already capturing opportunities in an opportunity backlog—a prioritized list of opportunities. They prioritize their list of customer needs, pain points, and desires the same way they prioritize their user stories in their development backlog.

This is a great place to start. It's better than working with only one opportunity at a time. However, it can be hard to prioritize a flat list of opportunities, because opportunities come in different shapes and sizes. Some opportunities are interrelated, while others are subsets of others.

If we continue with our streaming-entertainment example, we might start with the following list of opportunities:

- I can't find anything to watch.
- I'm out of episodes of my favorite shows.
- I can't figure out how to search for a specific show.
- I don't know when a new season is available.
- The show I was watching is no longer available.
- I fell asleep, and several episodes kept playing.
- I want to watch my shows on my flight.
- I want to skip the show intro.
- Is this show any good?
- I want to know what my friends are watching.
- Who is that actor?
- I want to watch my shows on my train commute.

I don't know how to compare "I can't find anything to watch" with "I'm out of episodes of my favorite shows." These opportunities are not distinct. Running out of episodes of your favorite show is a reason why you might not have anything to watch. But it's not the only reason, so these aren't exactly the same, either.

"I want to watch my shows on my flight" and "I want to watch my shows on my train commute" sound similar. Are these really the same opportunity? Maybe they can be combined into, "I want to watch on the go." That might be right. Unless planes and trains introduce different constraints. I may need to be completely offline on a plane, whereas, on a train, I may still have cell data. I might have access to a power outlet on a plane, but not on a train. If these context differences are important to the experience, these opportunities are similar, but not the same. But how do I prioritize them against each other? Can I address them both at the same time?

"Is this show any good?" feels like a big, hard problem. How do we evaluate "good" for each individual viewer? "Who is that actor?" feels much easier. Should we always prioritize easy over hard? If so, when do we ever get to the hard problems that have the potential to differentiate us from our competitors and really drive our outcomes?

It's hard to answer these questions when prioritizing opportunities of different shapes and sizes against each other. The opportunity space is too complex to manage as a flat list. Let's turn to a better alternative.

The Power of Trees

Instead of managing an opportunity backlog, we'll use an opportunity solution tree (introduced in Chapter 2) to help us map out and understand the opportunity space. The tree structure will help us visualize and understand the complexity of the opportunity space.

Trees depict two key relationships—parent-child relationships and sibling relationships. Both will help us make sense of the messy opportunity space. The parent-child relationship will be used to represent subsets—a child opportunity (or sub-opportunity) is a subset of a parent opportunity. For example, in the previous section, we saw that "I'm out of episodes of my favorite show" was one reason—but not the *only* reason—for "I can't find anything to watch." Referring to the tree relationships, we would say that "I can't find anything to watch" is the parent of the child "I'm out of episodes of my favorite shows."

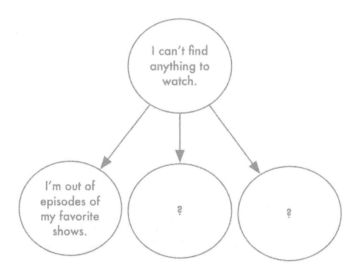

We might then ask, "What are some other reasons our customers say, 'I can't find anything to watch'?" We might add, "I can't figure out how to search for a specific show" and "The show I was watching is no longer available" as siblings to "I'm out of episodes of my favorite shows." Siblings should be similar to each other—in that they are each a subset of the same parent—but distinct in that you can address one without addressing another. For example, we can address "I can't figure out how to search for a specific show"

without addressing "I'm out of episodes of my favorite shows." But by addressing "I can't figure out how to search for a specific show," we partially address "I can't find anything to watch."

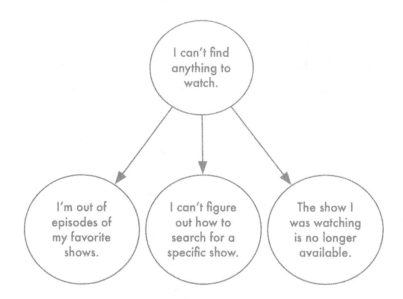

Sibling relationships help us make sense of similar opportunities like "I want to watch my shows on my flight" and "I want to watch my shows on my train commute." We can easily depict both on our tree under the parent opportunity "I want to watch my shows on the go." This allows us to treat each context (e.g., plane, train) as a specific need to address, while also visualizing the similarities. They are both sub-opportunities of the same parent.

When we learn to think in the structure of trees, it helps us deconstruct large, intractable problems into a series of smaller, more solvable problems. For example, "Is this show any good?" might, on the surface, look like a challenging problem to solve. But as we dig in and learn more, we realize that different people solve this problem in different ways. Some people choose what to watch based on the type of show (e.g., they like dramas or crime shows). Others choose shows based on who is in it—they have favorite actors—and they use the cast list as their primary selection factor. The more we learn about how people evaluate shows today, the more likely we can turn a big, intractable problem like "Is this show any good?" into a series of more solvable problems: "What type of show is this?" "Who is in this show?" "Is this show similar to another show I've watched?" "Who else is watching this show?" and so on. The big, intractable problem of "Is this show any good?" is a parent opportunity, while the rest are its sub-opportunities (or children).

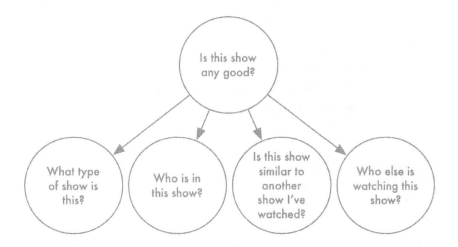

The value of breaking big opportunities into a series of smaller opportunities is twofold. First, it allows us to tackle problems that otherwise might seem unsolvable. And second, it allows us to deliver value over time. That second benefit is at the heart of the Agile manifesto and is a key tenet of continuous improvement. Rather than waiting until we can solve the bigger problem—"Is this show any good?"—we can deliver value iteratively over time. We might start by solving the smaller problem of "Who is in this show?" because it's fairly easy to solve and because we know a large percentage of our audience chooses shows according to this criterion. This allows us to ship value quickly. Now it might not solve the bigger opportunity completely, but it does solve a smaller need completely. Once we have accomplished that, we can move on to the next small opportunity. Over time, as we continuously ship value, we'll chip away at the larger opportunity. Eventually, we'll have solved enough of the smaller opportunities that we will, in turn, have solved the larger opportunity.

Additionally, the tree structure is going to be invaluable when it comes time to assessing and prioritizing opportunities. Our goal is to work on the most impactful opportunity, but we can't assess every opportunity we come across. We'd spend weeks assessing the opportunity space instead of shipping value to our customers. Instead, we'll use the tree structure to help us make fast decisions. We'll learn more about that in the next chapter.

For now, know that, while structuring the opportunity space is hard work, the effort will be paid back with hefty rewards.

Identifying Distinct Branches

To unlock the power of deconstructing big, intractable challenges into a series of more solvable, smaller opportunities, we need a well-structured opportunity space. A key concept that drives this structure is the idea of distinctness. We need each opportunity to be distinct from every other opportunity. If there's overlap, then we can't work on one at a time. Instead, they all get enmeshed with each other, and we need to work on all of them at the same time. If this is how you are feeling, it's a good sign that your tree needs more structure.

Working with product teams, I've identified two ways to uncover the underlying structure of your opportunity space. The first is to use the steps of your experience map that you created in Chapter 4. The second is to use your interview drawings to identify key moments in time. Both strategies accomplish the same goal—they help you organize the opportunity space by distinct moments so that there is no overlap from one branch to the next. We'll dive into both options in more detail here.

In Chapter 4, you learned how to visualize what you already know about your customers' experience. The output of this exercise was an experience map that showcases what your customers do to address their needs today. You learned that the map can help direct the stories that you collect in your interviews. It can also help give structure to the opportunity space. Our goal is to identify distinct moments in time during your customers' experience. Oftentimes this is as simple as mapping each node in your experience map to the top level of opportunities on your opportunity solution tree.

However, if your team isn't starting from a strong understanding of the customer experience, your map may not have distinct moments in time. It needs to evolve before you can identify them. Another approach to uncovering these distinct moments is to analyze the customer stories you are collecting in your interviews. In Chapter 5, I encouraged you to draw the stories that you heard. You do this by identifying the key moments in time that occurred during each story. If you take all of these drawings and start to label each key moment (or node), you'll notice patterns across your unique stories. What nodes are showing up in story after story? How can you stitch the most common nodes together to create an experience map that represents the set of stories that you are collecting? You can then map these nodes to your top-level opportunities.

With either strategy, the key is to make sure there is no overlap between the moments in time. Overlap will prevent us from working on one opportunity at a time. If we continue with our streaming-entertainment case study, we might identify the following distinct moments based on our experience map from Chapter 4:

- Deciding to watch something
- Choosing something to watch
- Watching something

- The end of the watching experience

From these distinct moments in time, we could then create the following top-level opportunities:

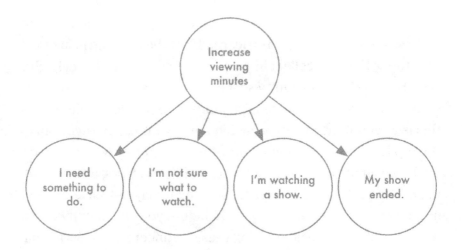

Take an Inventory of the Opportunity Space

With your distinct branches in place, we now want to take an inventory of the opportunities you have heard in your customer interviews. If you've been creating interview snapshots for each interview (as recommended in Chapter 5), you can simply review each interview snapshot. However, you don't want to add every opportunity to your tree. Instead, for each opportunity, ask the following questions:

- Is this opportunity framed as a customer need, pain point, or desire and not a solution?
- Is this opportunity unique to this customer, or have we seen it in more than one interview?
- If we address this opportunity, will it drive our desired outcome?

If the answer to all three of these questions is "Yes," you'll want to add it to your opportunity solution tree. For now, simply group it under the branch in which it occurs. If it seems like it could live under more than one branch, reframe the opportunity to be more specific. You may even need to split it into multiple opportunities, one for each moment in which it occurs, so that each can be grouped under their respective branches.

For example, "The interface is hard to use" is way too broad of an opportunity. We could boil the ocean trying to address every usability issue in our product. Instead, we want to get more specific. Where did this pain point show up in your customer's story? This may turn into several opportunities: "I can't figure out how to find a specific show that I have in mind," "I don't like entering a show name using the remote," or "I can't remember what episode I watched last." Each of these are more specific. They are easier problems to solve, and they now each live in only one spot on the tree.

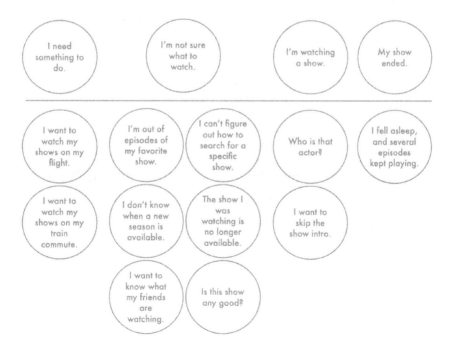

Add Structure to Each Branch

Now that you've collected the relevant opportunities, it's time to add structure to each branch. Work with one branch at a time. Start by grouping similar opportunities together. Similar opportunities might be siblings, like we saw with "I want to watch my shows on a plane" and "I want to watch my shows on my train commute." Or they might turn out to be the same opportunity worded slightly differently. For example, "I don't like entering a show title with my remote control" and "Selecting letters with the keypad is hard."

If your similar opportunities are siblings, look for a parent opportunity. In our train/plane example, we identified, "I want to watch my shows on the go" as the parent opportunity. This might have been explicitly mentioned in an interview, in which case, it will already be in our branch. But if it wasn't, it's fine to go ahead and add it, as it's implied by the other two opportunities. So, don't fret if you need to add parent opportunities that weren't explicitly stated in an interview.

If your similar opportunities are really the same, like we saw with the two opportunities about entering a show title with a remote, simply combine them into one opportunity. In this case, we might merge them into "Entering a show name into the search box is hard."

As you start to group siblings together and identify parent opportunities, you'll end up with a set of mini-trees. Look for sibling relationships between the parents of those mini-trees. Which can you group together? If you need to, add a shared parent to cluster similar opportunities together. Keep iterating through these steps until you've identified a set of siblings that ladder up to the top opportunity (i.e., the one that reflects a key moment) from which all other opportunities descend.

Then repeat the whole process for the remaining branches in your tree.

Just Enough Structure

One of the biggest challenges with opportunity mapping is that it looks deceptively simple. However, it does require quite a bit of critical thinking. You'll want to examine each opportunity to ensure it is properly framed, that you know what it means, and that it has the potential to drive your desired outcome. If you do your first tree in 30 minutes and think you are done, you are probably not thinking hard enough. However, I also see teams make the opposite mistake. They churn for hours trying to create the perfect tree. We don't want to do that, either.

The key is to find the sweet spot between giving you enough structure to see the big picture, but not so much that you are overwhelmed with detail. Unfortunately, it will take some experience to get this right, as it's a "You'll know it when you see it" type of situation.

But here's what I'll leave you with as you embark on mapping your first opportunity space. This isn't a one-and-done exercise. As Barbara Tversky says in the opening quote, "Structure is done, undone, and redone." You should be revisiting your opportunity solution tree often. You'll continue to reframe opportunities as you learn more about what they really mean. Seemingly simple opportunities will subdivide into myriad sub-opportunities as you start exploring them in your interviews. This is normal. You don't have to do all of this work in your first draft. Do just enough to capture what you currently know, and trust that it will continue to grow and evolve over time.

Avoid Common Anti-Patterns

After you've created your first draft, keep an eye out for these common anti-patterns.

Opportunities framed from your company's perspective. Product teams think about their product and business all day every day. It's easy to get stuck thinking from your company's perspective rather than your customers' perspective. However, if we want to be truly human-centered, solving customer needs while creating value for the business, we need to frame opportunities from our customers' perspective. No customer would ever say, "I wish I had more streaming-entertainment subscriptions." But they might say, "I want access to more compelling content." Review each opportunity on your tree and ask, "Have we heard this in interviews?" If you had to add opportunities to support the structure of your tree, you might ask, "Can I imagine a customer saying this?" Or are we just *wishing* a customer would say this?

Vertical opportunities. Vertical opportunities are when we have a parent with one child, who, in turn, has only one child, resulting in a vertical stack of single opportunities. Vertical opportunities tend to arise in two situations. One: You hear similar opportunities from several interviews, and each opportunity is really saying the same thing in different words. In this case, simply reframe one opportunity to encompass the broader need, and remove the rest. Otherwise, you're missing sibling opportunities. If each sub-opportunity only partially solves the parent, then identify which sibling opportunities are missing, and fill them in. If you aren't sure what the missing opportunities are, explore the parent opportunity in your upcoming interviews.

Opportunities have multiple parent opportunities. If your top-level opportunities represent distinct moments in time, then no opportunity should have two parents. If you are finding that an opportunity should ladder up to more than one parent, it's framed too broadly. Get more specific. Define one opportunity for each moment in time in which that need, pain point, or desire occurs.

Opportunities are not specific. Opportunities that represent themes, design guidelines, or even sentiment, aren't specific enough. "I wish this was easy to use," "This is too hard," and "I want to do everything on the go" are not good opportunities. However, if we make them more specific, they can become good opportunities: "I wish finding a show to watch was easier," "Entering a movie title using the remote is hard," and "I want to watch shows on my train commute" are great opportunities.

Opportunities are solutions in disguise. Often in an interview, your customer will ask for solutions. Sometimes they will even sound like opportunities. For example, you might hear a customer say, "I wish I could fast-forward through commercials." You might be tempted to capture this as an opportunity. However, this is really a solution request. The easiest way to distinguish between an opportunity and a solution is to ask, "Is there more than one way to address this opportunity?" In this example, the only way to allow people to fast-forward through commercials is to offer a fast-forward solution. This isn't an opportunity at all. Instead, we want to uncover the implied opportunity. Maybe it's as simple as, "I don't like commercials." Why does this reframing help? If we then ask, "How might we address 'I don't like commercials'?" we can generate several options. We can create more entertaining commercials—like those we see during the Super Bowl. We can allow you to fast-forward through commercials like the customer suggested. Or we can offer a commercial-free subscription. An opportunity should have more than one potential solution. Otherwise, it's simply a solution in disguise.

Capturing feelings as opportunities. When a customer expresses emotion in an interview, it's usually a strong signal that an opportunity is lurking nearby. However, don't capture the feeling itself as the opportunity. Instead, look for the *cause* of the feeling. When we capture opportunities like "I'm frustrated" or "I'm overwhelmed," we limit how we can help. We can't fix feelings. But if we capture the *cause* of those feelings—"I hate typing in my password every time I purchase a show" or "I'm way behind on this show"—we can often identify solutions that address the underlying cause. So, do note when a customer expresses a feeling, but consider it a signpost, and remember to let it direct you to the underlying opportunity.

CHAPTER SEVEN

PRIORITIZING OPPORTUNITIES, NOT SOLUTIONS

"The build trap is when organizations become stuck measuring their success by outputs rather than outcomes. It's when they focus more on shipping and developing features rather than on the actual value those things produce."
— Melissa Perri

"When people create maps of an unknowable, unpredictable world, they face strong temptations toward either overconfident knowing or overly cautious doubt. Wisdom consists of an attitude toward one's beliefs, values, knowledge, and information that resists these temptations through an ongoing balance between knowing and doubt."
— Karl Weick

I'm standing on the stage at Davies Symphony Hall in San Francisco, looking out at a sea of product people. I'm wrapping up a talk about how product teams can manage stakeholders throughout the discovery process. It's the last talk of the day at Mind the Product. All we have left is the after-party, and I want to leave the crowd with an important takeaway. "You are never one feature away from success..." The crowd erupts with cheers.

But I'm not done. I wait patiently for the crowd to quiet down. I continue, "...and you never will be." The energy in the room is electric. I know people need to hear it, but I also know that saying it isn't enough.

For too long, product teams have defined their work as shipping the next release. When we engage with stakeholders, we talk about our roadmaps and our backlogs. During our performance reviews, we highlight all the great features we implemented. The vast majority of our conversations take place in the solution space. We assume that success comes from launching features. This is what product thought leader Melissa Perri calls "the build trap."[28]

This obsession with producing outputs is strangling us. It's why we spend countless hours prioritizing features, grooming backlogs, and micro-managing releases. The hard reality is that product strategy doesn't happen in the solution space. Our customers don't care about the majority of our feature releases. A solution-first mindset is good at producing output, but it rarely produces outcomes.

Instead, our customers care about solving their needs, pain points, and desires. Product strategy happens in the opportunity space. Strategy emerges from the decisions we make about which outcomes to pursue, customers to serve, and opportunities to address. Sadly, the vast majority of product teams rush past these decisions and jump straight to prioritizing features. We obsess about the competition instead of about our customers. Our strategy consists of playing catch-up, and, no matter how hard we work, we always seem to fall further and further behind.

Fortunately, there's a better way. With a well-structured opportunity space (see Chapter 6), a product trio is now well positioned to make strategic decisions about which opportunities to address,

---

28 See Melissa Perri's *Escaping the Build Trap: How Effective Product Management Creates Real Value*

which customers to serve, and which path to take toward their desired outcome. This chapter will show you how.

Focus on One Target Opportunity at a Time

In the Opportunity Mapping chapter (Chapter 6), you learned that, as you work vertically down the opportunity solution tree, you are deconstructing large, intractable opportunities into a series of smaller, more solvable sub-opportunities. The benefit of this work is that it helps us adopt an Agile mindset, working iteratively, delivering value over time, rather than delivering a large project after an extended period of time.

By addressing only one opportunity at a time, we unlock the ability to deliver value iteratively over time. If we spread ourselves too thin across many opportunities, we'll find ourselves right back in the waterfall mindset of taking too long to deliver too much all at once. Instead, we want to solve one opportunity before moving on to the next.

Focusing on one opportunity at a time allows the trio to explore multiple solutions (more on that in Chapter 8), setting up good compare-and-contrast decisions. It's also consistent with the *kanban* concept of limiting work in progress. Researchers at the University of Oulu in Finland conducted a literature review on the benefits of *kanban* and found that software teams that use *kanban* see an increase in quality and consistency in delivery and a decrease in customer complaints. They found that limiting work in progress was a key component of this success[29].

To choose a target opportunity, you'll need to assess and prioritize the opportunity space. However, you don't need to assess every

---

29   M. O. Ahmad, J. Markkula and M. Oivo, *"Kanban* in software development: A systematic literature review," 2013 39th Euromicro Conference on Software Engineering and Advanced Applications, Santander, 2013, pp. 9–16, doi: 10.1109/SEAA.2013.28.

opportunity you encounter. Instead, you'll use the tree structure to help you optimize your prioritization.

Using the Tree to Aid Decision Making

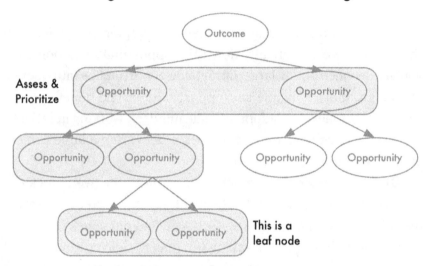

You'll start by assessing your top-level opportunities—the parent opportunities on your opportunity solution tree. Drawing from what we learned in Chapter 2, you won't be working with each top-level opportunity in isolation. You don't want to ask, "Should we pursue this opportunity?" That's a "whether or not" question that leads to poor decisions. It makes us susceptible to confirmation bias, and we forget to consider opportunity cost. Instead, you'll compare and contrast the set of parent opportunities against each other.

In the next section, we'll explore how to best assess sets of opportunities. For now, assume you can identify the highest priority. If your opportunity space is well structured (see Chapter 6), you can now ignore all but this branch of the tree for the rest of your assessment. If your chosen parent is the highest priority, then the highest-impact opportunity to address next will live under that branch.

Notice how a single decision, assessing and prioritizing your top-level opportunities, reduces the amount of assessing you have to do. We can effectively ignore the other branches of our tree and focus on assessing just our target branch. That's the power of the tree structure.

We'll now repeat our assessing-and-prioritizing exercise for the children of our primary top-level opportunity. We'll compare and contrast the children against each other and choose a front runner. If our front runner has children, we'll repeat the exercise again. We'll keep iterating until we identify a target opportunity that has no children.

You always want to choose a leaf-node opportunity (i.e., one that has no children) because our goal is to deliver iterative value over time. We can do this by solving a series of smaller opportunities in succession rather than addressing sets of opportunities at once. However, this doesn't necessarily mean that your target opportunity will be easy to address. It simply means that you haven't (yet) identified any sub-opportunities that contribute to addressing it.

Assessing a Set of Opportunities

I recommend that teams assess opportunities using the following criteria: opportunity sizing, market factors, company factors, and customer factors.

Opportunity sizing helps us answer the questions: How many customers are affected and how often? However, we don't need to size each opportunity precisely. This can quickly turn into a never-ending data-gathering mission. Instead, we want to size a set of siblings against each other. For each set that we are considering, we want to ask, "Which of these opportunities affects the most customers?" and "the most often?" We can and should make rough estimates here. You can use behavioral data (e.g., site analytics, sales-funnel analytics), support tickets, sample surveys, or even your interview snapshots, to quickly evaluate which opportunities are impacting the most customers.

It's important, however, to distinguish *how many* customers from *how often*. Every customer might be impacted by an opportunity, but the need or pain point might arise only occasionally. Addressing this opportunity will have a different impact than addressing an opportunity that impacts *some* customers *all the time*.

Market factors help us evaluate how addressing each opportunity might affect our position in the market. Depending on the competitive landscape, some opportunities might be table stakes, while others might be strategic differentiators. Choosing one over the other will depend on your current position in the market. A missing table stake could torpedo sales, while a strategic differentiator could open up new customer segments. The key is to consider how addressing each opportunity positions you against your competitors. With market factors, we also want to consider any external trends (both opportunities and threats) that might impact which opportunity we might choose.[30] For example, our streaming-entertainment company might want to consider the impact of "cord-cutters" (i.e., the growing trend of cable subscribers canceling their service) on different opportunities. They might prioritize an opportunity like "I want to watch live sports" to grab some of this market.

Company factors help us evaluate the strategic impact of each opportunity for our company, business group, or team. Each organizational context is unique. Google might choose to address an opportunity that Apple would never touch. We need to consider our organizational context when assessing and prioritizing opportunities. We want to prioritize opportunities that support our company vision, mission, and strategic objectives over opportunities that

---

30 For a good way to assess external trends, see this explanation of STEEP analysis: http://www.utsdesignindex.com/researchmethod/steep-analysis/

don't. We want to de-prioritize opportunities that conflict with our company values. We also want to consider the company's political climate. We might need to spend a lot of political capital to gain support for a more controversial opportunity. If we aren't willing to do that, we'll want to choose another opportunity.

Company factors also apply at the business-group and team level. A business group might be your business unit, your department, your tribe, or even your product line. Your business group's vision, mission, and strategic objectives might add additional constraints on what you may or may not choose. These same factors might apply at your team or squad level as well.

Across all three levels—company, business group, and team— you'll also want to consider strengths and weaknesses. Some companies will be better positioned to tackle some opportunities over others. Some teams may have unique skills that give them an unfair advantage when tackling a specific opportunity. We want to take all of this into account when assessing and prioritizing opportunities.

Customer factors help us evaluate how important each opportunity is to our customers. If we interviewed and opportunity mapped well, every opportunity on our tree will represent a real customer need, pain point, or desire. However, not all opportunities are equally important to customers. We'll want to assess how important each opportunity is to our customers and how satisfied they are with existing solutions.[31] We want to prioritize important opportunities where satisfaction with the current solution is low, over opportunities that are less important or where satisfaction with current opportunities is high.

---

31 I first read about this importance/satisfaction matrix in Dan Olsen's *The Lean Product Playbook*. However, the earliest origin of the idea I can find is this academic paper: Chen, Shun-Hsing; Yang, Ching-Chow; Lin, Wen-Tsann; and Yeh, Tsu-Ming. (2007). Service quality attributes determine improvement priority. *The Tqm Magazine*. 19. 162–175. 10.1108/09544780710730005.

Embrace the Messiness

You might be tempted to score each opportunity based on the different factors (e.g., 2 out of 3 for sizing, 1 out of 3 for market factors, and so on) and then stack-rank your opportunities, much like you might do with features. Don't do this. This is a messy, subjective decision, and you want to keep it that way.

Remember, you aren't making absolute judgments. You are making relative judgments by comparing and contrasting sibling opportunities against each other. You don't need to score each opportunity. This will take a lot of work, will be rife with assumptions, and won't lead to a better decision. Instead, make a data-informed, subjective comparison for each set of factors.

There may not be a clear winner, and that's okay. One opportunity might look like the winner based on sizing, and another might look like the winner based on company factors. Yet another might look like the winner based on customer factors. Your job as a team is to have a healthy debate. Consider the different dimensions, and make the best decision that you can for this moment in time. Think about each set of criteria as a different lens through which to view impact. Use the lenses to fuel your conversation.

When we turn a subjective, messy decision into a quantitative math formula, we are treating an ill-structured problem as if it were a well-structured problem. The problem with this strategy is that it will lead us to believe that there is one true, right answer. And there isn't. Once we mathematize this process, we'll stop thinking and go strictly by the numbers. We don't want to do this.

Instead, we want to leave room for doubt. As Karl Weick, an educational psychologist at the University of Michigan, advises in the second opening quote, wisdom is finding the right balance between having confidence in what you know and leaving enough room for doubt in case you are wrong.[32] That's the balance we are looking for here. When we treat this like the messy, subjective decision that it is, we are leaving room for doubt, so that, down the road, if we learn we are addressing the wrong opportunity, we will be far more likely to course-correct.

Two-Way Door Decisions

When assessing and prioritizing the opportunity space, it's important that we find the right balance between being data-informed and not getting stuck in analysis paralysis. It's easy to fall into the trap of wanting more data, spending just a little bit more time, trying to get to a more perfect decision. However, we'll learn more by making a decision and then seeing the consequences of having made that decision than we will from trying to think our way to the perfect decision.

Jeff Bezos, founder and CEO of Amazon, made this exact argument in his 2015 letter to shareholders,[33] where he introduced the idea of Level 1 and Level 2 decisions. He describes a Level 1 decision as one that is hard to reverse, whereas a Level 2 decision is one that is easy to reverse. Bezos argues that we should be slow and cautious when making Level 1 decisions, but that we should move fast and not wait for perfect data when making Level 2 decisions.

I prefer the imagery of one-way door and two-way door decisions. With a one-way door decision, the idea is that, when we make the decision, we walk through the door. Upon entering the space on the other side of the door, we are able to see the consequences

---

32   See the Chapter "The Attitude of Wisdom: Ambivalence as the Optimal Compromise" in the book *Organizational Wisdom and Executive Courage*, edited by Suresh Srivastva and David L. Cooperrider.

33   See: http://bit.ly/2-way-door

of our decisions. Unfortunately, because it's a one-way door, if we don't like what we see, we can't turn around and walk out through the door again. This is what Bezos calls a "Level 1 decision." For these types of decisions, we want to be cautious, data-driven, and deliberate in our decision-making.

With a two-way door decision, on the other hand, when we walk through the door, if we don't like what we see, we get to turn around and undo our decision. This is what Bezos calls a "Level 2 decision." He suggests that, with a two-way door decision, we'll learn more by acting—walking through the door and seeing what's on the other side—than we would by trying to *imagine* what's on the other side of the door.

When we assess and prioritize the opportunity space, even though these are some of the most strategic decisions we make as a product trio, we are still making two-way door decisions. When you choose a target opportunity, you are choosing how to spend your next few days or weeks. You are not committing to addressing that opportunity. You are simply committing to exploring it further with your discovery work. If, as you proceed to explore solutions, you learn that this wasn't the best decision (e.g., you learned something new, you found the solutions to be tougher than you imagined, you learned it wasn't as important to customers as you thought), you'll simply turn around and choose another target opportunity.

It's important that we frame our discovery decisions as two-way door, reversible decisions. Lottie Bullens and colleagues, social psychologists at the University of Amsterdam, found in a series of studies that, when people viewed a decision as reversible, they continued to critically evaluate their decision after making it. In fact, they were more likely to see the negative attributes of their choice and the positive attributes of the alternatives after making the decision if they viewed it as a reversible decision. If they framed it as an irreversible decision, the opposite happened. People noticed only the positive attributes of their own choice and the negative attributes of the alternatives.[34] If we want to stay open to being wrong and avoid confirmation bias, it's critical that we think of our prioritization decisions as reversible decisions.

The beauty of a continuous discovery process is that we can always course-correct as we learn. So, as you assess and prioritize the opportunity space, relax. Make the best decision you can, given what you know today, and know that, if you got it wrong, we'll simply revisit the decision when we need to.

Avoid These Common Anti-Patterns

As you assess and prioritize the opportunity space, be sure to avoid these common anti-patterns.

Delaying a decision until there is more data. Even when I remind teams that choosing a target opportunity is a two-way door decision and that, if all of the opportunities on your tree emerged from customer interviews, there are no wrong decisions, some teams *still* get bogged down in the data. They want to look into *one more thing*. Wait for *one more data report*. Ask *one more person* for input. The intent is good. We do want to be data-informed. But we also want to move forward. We'll learn more from testing our decisions than we will from trying to make perfect decisions. The best way to prevent this type of analysis paralysis is to time-box your decision. Give yourself an hour or two or, at most, a day or two. Then decide, based on what you know today, and move on. Trust that you'll course-correct if you get data down the road that tells you that you made a less-than-optimal decision.

Over-relying on one set of factors at the cost of the others. Some teams are all about opportunity sizing. Others focus

---

34   Bullens, L., van Harreveld, F., Förster, J., and van der Pligt, J. (2013). "Reversible decisions: The grass isn't merely greener on the other side; it's also very brown over here." *Journal of Experimental Social Psychology*, 49(6), 1093–1099. https://doi.org/10.1016/j.jesp.2013.07.011

exclusively on what's most important to their customers. Many teams forget to consider company factors and choose opportunities that will never get organizational buy-in. The four sets of factors (opportunity sizing, market factors, company factors, and customer factors) are designed to be lenses to give you a different perspective on the decision. Use them all.

Working backwards from your expected conclusion. Some teams go into this exercise with a conclusion in mind. As a result, they don't use the lenses to explore the possibilities and instead use them to justify their foregone conclusion. This is a waste of time. Go into this exercise with an open mind. You'll be surprised by how often you come away from it with a new perspective.

DISCOVERING SOLUTIONS

In this section, we'll explore how to generate, evaluate, and iterate on the solutions that will help you create customer value and business value. You'll learn how to:

- Ideate effectively so that you can embrace a "compare and contrast" mindset and work with sets of solutions rather than fixating on your favorite solution (Chapter 8).
- Identify the hidden assumptions that are lurking behind each of your ideas, helping you catch blind spots before they can negatively impact your solutions (Chapter 9).
- Test assumptions in a way that helps you quickly throw out what's not working and iterate on what is (Chapter 10).

CHAPTER EIGHT

SUPERCHARGED IDEATION

"Creative teams know that quantity is the best predictor of quality."
— Leigh Thompson, *Making the Team*

*"You'll never stumble upon the unexpected
if you stick only to the familiar."*
— Ed Catmull, *Creativity, Inc.*

You've identified a clear customer need, pain point, or desire—your target opportunity—and it's finally time to jump into the solution space. Where do you start? For many, the answer is brainstorming. Now, odds are you just had one of two reactions when you read that. Either you conjured an image of a lively group standing before a wall of multi-colored stickies, laughing, sharing ideas, essentially having fun. Or you conjured an image of a windowless conference room with a few people shouting out ideas and one person scribing at the whiteboard while everyone else looks bored.

At some companies, brainstorming is defined as the be-all-end-all, the panacea from which all good ideas emerge. For others, it's the epitome of a Dilbert comic—a complete waste of everyone's time. In the first case, participants argue it's the most effective tool in their toolbox and is responsible for all of their creative success.

In the second case, participants are skeptical that any good could come of this exercise. What's going on here? Why is brainstorming so polarizing? Does it work? Why or why not? In this chapter, we'll tackle all of these questions and much more.

Quantity Leads to Quality

For many of us, brainstorming seems unnecessary. We hear about a customer problem or need, and our brain immediately jumps to a solution. It's human nature. We are good at closing the loop—we hear about a problem, and our brain wants to solve it. However, creativity research tells us that our first idea is rarely our best idea. Researchers measure creativity using three primary criteria: fluency (the number of ideas we generate), flexibility (how diverse the ideas are), and originality (how novel an idea is).[35]

Similar research shows that fluency is correlated with both flexibility and originality.[36] In other words, as we generate more ideas, the diversity and novelty of those ideas increases. Additionally, the most original ideas tend to be generated toward the end of the ideation session.[37] They weren't the first ideas we came up with. So even though our brain is very good at generating fast solutions, we want to learn to keep the loop open longer. We want to learn to push beyond our first mediocre and obvious ideas, and delve into the realm of more diverse, original ideas.

Most product teams are inundated with too many ideas. We have endless backlogs, countless customer requests, and a never-ending

---

35 Guilford, J. P. 1959. *Personality*. New York: McGraw-Hill; also Guilford, J. P., 1967. *The Nature of Human Intelligence*. New York: McGraw-Hill.

36 Paulus, Paul & Kohn, Nicholas & Arditti, Lauren. (2011). "Effects of Quantity and Quality Instructions on Brainstorming." *The Journal of Creative Behavior*. 45. 10.1002/j.2162-6057.2011.tb01083.x.

37 Basadur, M. and Thompson, R. (1986), "Usefulness of the Ideation Principle of Extended Effort in Real World Professional and Managerial Creative Problem Solving". *The Journal of Creative Behavior*, 20: 23–34. doi:10.1002/j.2162-6057.1986.tb00414.x

roadmap. The problem, however, is that many of these ideas are first ideas to a variety of customer opportunities.

If we took the time to map each item in our backlog, each customer request, and each initiative on our roadmap to the opportunities on our opportunity solution tree (see Chapters 2 and 6), odds are we'll have only one or two solutions for each opportunity. Even though we are inundated with ideas, we aren't pushing past our first or second mediocre ideas to get to the realm of diverse and original ideas.

Now, not all opportunities need an innovative solution. You don't need to reinvent the "forgot password" workflow (but you should still test it—more on that in Chapter 11). But for the strategic opportunities where you want to differentiate from your competitors, you'll want to take the time to generate several ideas to ensure that you uncover the best ones.

Okay, so let's get everyone in a room to brainstorm so that we can find those more diverse and original ideas, right? Not quite. We first need to discuss the challenges with brainstorming.

The Problem With Brainstorming

Brainstorming was introduced and popularized by Alex Osborn, an executive at a respected advertising firm, in his 1953 book *Applied Imagination*. He believed brainstorming was the lynchpin underlying creativity and wanted to share his company's process with the world. To help put this book into context, it's similar to what we see today with Ed Catmull's book *Creativity, Inc.* about Pixar's creative process or Tom Kelley's *The Art of Innovation* about how the leading design firm IDEO works. Like Pixar and IDEO today, people admired Osborn's creative success, and brainstorming spread quickly.

Osborn outlined four rules for brainstorming. One, focus on quantity. In other words, generate as many ideas as you can. Two, defer judgment, and separate idea generation from idea evaluation. Three, welcome unusual ideas. And four, combine and improve ideas. He suggested that groups come together real-time, face-to-face (remember he predated the digital, asynchronous communication tools we have today), to generate ideas together, using these four rules. For those of you who have participated in brainstorming sessions, these rules aren't new. They are still in common use today.

As brainstorming rose in popularity, academic researchers started to question if it worked. Was brainstorming in groups the most effective way to generate ideas? For decades researchers ran studies in which they compared the creative output of brainstorming groups against the creative output of the same number of individuals generating ideas alone. Study after study found that the individuals generating ideas alone outperformed the brainstorming groups. Individuals generated more ideas, more diverse ideas, and more original ideas.[38]

As researchers dug into why individuals outperformed groups, they identified four mitigating factors. First, research has found that people tend to work harder when working individually than when working in groups. This is called social loafing. When we are on our own, we have no choice but to put in the work, whereas when we are in a group, we can rely on the efforts of others.

Second, brainstorming groups exhibited many of the common challenges associated with group conformity. The early ideas set the tone for later ideas. Ideas were often too conservative or similar to each other. Members censored their ideas due to concerns about how others would judge their ideas.

Third, brainstorming groups ran into challenges with production blocking—that's a fancy term for a simple idea. Have you ever been about to say something when someone else jumped in, prompting

38 Brian Mullen, Craig Johnson & Eduardo Salas (1991) "Productivity Loss in Brainstorming Groups: A Meta-Analytic Integration," *Basic and Applied Social Psychology*, 12:1, 3–23, DOI: 10.1207/s15324834basp1201_1

you to forget what you were going to say? That's production block-ing. In group brainstorming sessions, people lose ideas amid the chaos of everyone sharing ideas in rapid succession.

And finally, the fourth factor is a common group trait known as downward norm setting—the performance of the group tends to be limited to the lowest-performing member. Rather than the strongest member raising everyone else up, the opposite happens. The weakest member brings everyone else down. These factors combined to inhibit the performance of the brainstorming groups as compared to the individuals who generated ideas alone.[39]

This raises the question: Why are brainstorming advocates so adamant that brainstorming works? It turns out researchers have an answer to this question as well. Bernard Nijstad and colleagues at the University of Groningen in the Netherlands found that brain-storming groups are subject to what they call "the illusion of group productivity."[40] This is a phenomenon in which groups overestimate their performance. They also report high levels of satisfaction with their work despite their lesser performance.

Nijstad and colleagues attribute this overestimation to a reduc-tion in cognitive failures. They define a "cognitive failure" as occurring when a participant can't generate any ideas. When you are brainstorming alone, you generate more cognitive failures than when you are brainstorming in a group. Ideas from the group help other group members get unstuck.

But even with this group advantage, individuals generating ideas alone still generated more ideas, more diverse ideas, and more orig-inal ideas than brainstorming groups. The individuals simply had to work harder to get there. However, since the brainstorming groups spent less time stuck, their perception was that their performance

39   See Leigh Thompson's *Making the Team* for a good summary of this research.
40   Nijstad, Bernard and Stroebe, Wolfgang and Lodewijkx, Hein. (2006). "The illusion of group productivity: A reduction of failures explanation." *European Journal of Social Psychology*. 36. 31–48. 10.1002/ejsp.295.

was higher. This illusion of group productivity may explain why so many brainstorming advocates consider it a panacea.

So, if we stick to what the research tells us, individuals generating ideas on their own do outperform brainstorming groups. Even if we think brainstorming is effective, we are probably falling prey to the illusion of group productivity. Working in a group feels easier, so we think we must be performing at a higher level. Now, if you are wondering if there is a way to get the benefit of reducing cognitive failures that we see in groups with the creative output of individuals brainstorming on their own, it turns out there is.

Runa Korde and Paul Paulus, researchers at the University of Texas-Arlington, ran a series of studies that showed alternating between individual ideation and group sharing of ideas can improve the quality of ideas generated in subsequent individual ideation sessions.[41] Exposure to other people's ideas did inspire new ideas.

The key difference here is that individuals still generated ideas on their own. Participants started by ideating on their own. Then they shared their ideas with the group. Then they went back to ideating on their own. They never ideated as a group, but they received the benefit of hearing each other's ideas. You'll see in the methods described below that we'll be putting this same pattern into practice.

Getting Unstuck

When generating ideas on your own, it's only a matter of time before you'll get stuck. Generating ideas is hard work and takes effort. The first thing to recognize when you get stuck is that it happens to everyone. You aren't bad at generating ideas. You are creative.

---

41 Korde R., Paulus P. (2016) "Alternating individual and group idea generation: Finding the elusive synergy." *Journal of Experimental Social Psychology* Volume 70, May 2017, Pages 177–190

Many of us have self-limiting beliefs around creativity. We believe because we can't draw, paint, or play a musical instrument, we must not be creative. I'm here to tell you, you are. Creativity is a universal human trait. And as a product-team member, there is no one better than you to generate creative solutions to your customers' problems. If it's been a while since you've generated ideas, it might be slow to start. That's normal. Push through the discomfort and keep thinking. The following tips will help.

First, don't try to spend an hour generating ideas. Take frequent breaks. Spread it out throughout your day. Try to generate ideas in the few minutes you have between meetings. After lunch, go for a walk, and daydream about what you might build. A change of scenery can often inspire new ideas. Try generating ideas at different times of the day. Some of us will be better first thing in the morning, when we have a lot of mental energy; others might find the late afternoon to be the optimal idea-generation time. Experiment. Find what works best for you.

In addition to ideating at different times and in different places, take advantage of incubation.[42] Incubation occurs when your brain continues to consider a problem even after you've stopped consciously thinking about it. You've probably experienced this often in your life. After working on what seems like an unsolvable challenge all day, you finally go home and take a break. After a good night's sleep, you come to work, returning to the problem. Instantly, you identify a solution. In fact, it's hard to imagine why it seemed like such a hard problem yesterday. That's incubation. And it works. Incubation can be particularly helpful after hearing other people's ideas. You may not think of new ideas right away, but odds are, your brain is still working on it in the background. So, if you get stuck, sleep on it. Tomorrow will likely bring fresh ideas.

---

42   Sio, U. N., & Ormerod, T. C. (2009). "Does incubation enhance problem solving? A meta-analytic review." *Psychological Bulletin*, 135(1), 94–120. https://doi-org.turing.library.northwestern.edu/10.1037/a0014212

Another common way of getting unstuck is to look to analogous products for inspiration. For many product teams, this means competitive research. You should draw inspiration from your competitors, but look broader than that. Many innovative ideas come from unrelated domains. For example, Velcro was invented after the inventor found a cocklebur in his sock. He was intrigued by how the latching mechanism worked, and it inspired the design of Velcro.

When you get stuck, start with your competition. But then look wider. Ask yourself: What other industries have solved similar problems? They don't need to be similar or even be in an adjacent industry. You are looking for similarities in the target opportunity. For example, if you work for a job board and you are helping recruiters evaluate job candidates, you can look at other job boards, but you can also look at how online shopping sites help shoppers evaluate products, you can look at how travel aggregators help travelers choose hotels, and you can look at how insurance companies present different policies. These industries are unrelated to each other, but they are each solving analogous problems.

Additionally, when you are stuck, you can start to consider what your extreme users might need. What would a power user want? What does the first-time user need? What about people with different disabilities? How about people who live in remote locations or bustling cities? Young people? Senior citizens? Your extreme users will vary by product, but thinking about the needs of different types of users as they relate to your target opportunity can help you generate more ideas that may work for everyone.

And finally, don't be afraid to consider wild ideas. Some people don't like this suggestion, because wild ideas are rarely pursued. But wild ideas can improve more feasible ideas. This is where the power of mixing and matching different solutions to identify even-better ideas comes into play. So, when ideating, pretend you have a magic wand—anything is possible.

Putting It All Into Practice

Enough theory. Let's put some of these ideas into practice.

1. Review your target opportunity. Make sure that everyone on your team knows what it means and is familiar with the necessary context. Make sure it's distinct from the other opportunities that you've discussed and that it's an appropriately sized leaf-node opportunity. If you need to revisit any of these concepts, review the prior chapter before continuing.

2. Generate ideas alone. Take some time to jot down as many ideas as you can. When you get stuck, take a break, and come back to it. If you are still stuck, try to find inspiration from your competitors and analogous products. For analogous products, think broadly. You aren't limited to just the other players in your space.

3. Share ideas across your team. You can do this in a face-to-face, real-time meeting, or you can do it asynchronously in a digital chat channel (e.g., Slack or Microsoft Teams). The key is to take the time to describe each of your ideas, allow people to ask questions, and to riff on the ideas.

4. Repeat steps 2 and 3. Remember, the benefit of sharing your ideas is that hearing other people's ideas will inspire even more ideas. So, don't skip repeating step 2 to ensure that you reap the rewards. Repeat until you've generated between 15 and 20 ideas for your target opportunity. Remember, research shows that your first ideas are rarely your best ideas. The goal is to push your creative output to find the more diverse and more original ideas.

Evaluating Your Ideas

Once you've generated 15 to 20 ideas for the same target opportunity, it's time to start evaluating your ideas. First, start by asking for each, "Does this idea solve the target opportunity?" It's okay if it's only a partial solution, but you'll be surprised to find several ideas that don't solve your target opportunity at all. Don't worry—this is a natural side effect of idea generation. But now is the time to weed them out.

Next, you'll "dot-vote"[43] as a team to whittle your set down from lots of ideas to three ideas. Dot voting is a simple method that facilitates group evaluation. Research shows that while we are better at generating ideas individually, we are better at evaluating ideas as a group.[44] To dot-vote, allot three votes per member. As you vote, the only criteria you should be considering is how well the idea addresses the target opportunity. You aren't voting for the coolest, shiniest ideas. Nor are you ruling out the hardest or even impossible ideas. We'll deal with that down the road. Each person can assign their votes however they please. They can place all three votes on one idea or vote for three ideas individually. Once everyone has placed their votes, you'll select the top three ideas that garnered the most votes.

It may take a few rounds of dot-voting to get to your top three. For example, if after round one of voting, several ideas have one or two votes, but no ideas have three or more votes, take some time to discuss your votes. Don't let this turn into a long debate or argument. Instead, let each person pitch the ideas they voted for. During your pitch, be sure to highlight why each idea best addresses the target opportunity. Then vote again.

Coming out of any voting round, if there's a clear winner, set it aside as one of your three to move forward with. Continue dot-voting until you have set aside three ideas. It's important after you are done dot-voting to take a quick poll and make sure everyone on the team is excited about the set you are moving forward with. This doesn't mean you have to have consensus on all three options. But

---

43 Dot voting is a quick way to poll a group's opinion. Each person gets a set number of votes to distribute across the options as they see fit. The options with the most votes win.

44 See Leigh Thompson's *Making the Team*

everyone on the team should be excited about at least one idea, and each idea should have a strong advocate in the group. If that's not the case, revisit your set of ideas, and dot-vote again.

Dot-voting is a great way to go from lots of ideas down to some ideas. Groups tend to evaluate ideas better than individuals because groups have a wider breadth of experience to draw on. However, we don't want to dot-vote to select one idea. You'll see in the coming chapters that we will use prototyping and assumption testing to whittle our set down from three to one. Our goal for now is to set up a good compare-and-contrast decision: Which of these three ideas best delivers on our target opportunity? You'll learn how to answer that question with the next couple of habits.

Avoid These Common Anti-Patterns

As you generate ideas, be sure to avoid these common anti-patterns:

Not including diverse perspectives. Most of the exercises in this book are designed for product trios to do together. However, ideation is best done with the entire team. You want to make sure everyone has a chance to contribute their ideas. You also might consider inviting key stakeholders who bring a different perspective. The more diversity in the group, the more diverse ideas you'll generate. However, make sure that you set the context for ideation by sharing your target opportunity and the customer context in which that opportunity occurs.

Generating too many variations of the same idea. When we get stuck generating ideas, we tend to riff on variations of the same idea. If we try to list as many types of animals as possible, once we identify lions and tigers, we might add pumas, cheetahs, and snow leopards. This can be a good tactic for increasing the number of ideas that you generate. However, when selecting three to be in your consideration set, you want as much diversity as possible.

So, this can't be the only way that you generate ideas. Instead, deliberately work to identify categorically different ideas. If you get stuck, look for inspiration from analogous products. Analogous products don't need to be from your industry. In fact, the further away they are from your industry, the more likely you'll uncover diverse ideas. So, ask, "Who else has to solve a problem like this?" and then investigate how they solve it.

Limiting ideation to one session. Hosting a brainstorming meeting is a common business norm. We expect to generate ideas in one sitting. But research on generating ideas shows this isn't the most effective tactic. Instead, give ideation the time it deserves. Let your ideators consider ideas over time. Take advantage of the brain's innate ability to incubate a problem.

Selecting ideas that don't address the target opportunity. When ideating, you want to encourage your participants to defer judgment. As a result, it's not uncommon to end up with solutions that don't address your target opportunity. Before dot-voting, remove any ideas that don't address your target opportunity. Otherwise, it can be easy to get distracted by a shiny idea that might be a good idea for some day in the future but isn't a good idea right now. In the previous chapter, you made a strategic decision when you chose a target opportunity. Don't undo that work now.

CHAPTER NINE

IDENTIFYING HIDDEN ASSUMPTIONS

"We loosely define an iteration in discovery as trying out at least one new idea or approach...To set your expectations, teams competent in modern discovery techniques can generally test on the order of 10–20 iterations per week."
— Marty Cagan, *INSPIRED*

"Just assume that you are being overconfident, and give yourself a healthy margin of error."
— Chip and Dan Heath, *Decisive*

I was reading the news one morning when I encountered a story about an affordable housing project in Portland, Oregon (where I live). For decades, the city invested in gentrification policies that resulted in the displacement of many underserved families from Portland's historically Black neighborhood. To try to rectify the damage done, the city invested millions of dollars into a condominium building designed to help some of these displaced families return to their neighborhood.

The article, however, was critical of the project. Even though the city worked with the developer, granting tax breaks in exchange for offering the condos at below market rate, and the condos were available only to displaced residents, the displaced families were not opting to buy the condos. Years into the project, long after the city had estimated the building would be at full capacity, most units were not sold. In the end, the city had no choice but to let the developer sell the units on the open market.

This story upset me. Tens of millions of dollars of taxpayers' money was spent, with little impact. The city council had the best of intentions and tried to do the right thing, but the impact of their project fell short. Why did this happen?

The answer is simple. The city council and the real estate developer made a number of assumptions about what displaced families wanted for housing, and neither thought to test those assumptions. The developer built a building consisting primarily of one- and two-bedroom units. Both the city council and the developer thought this was how they could maximize impact and help the most families. Unfortunately, most of the displaced families were families of four or more. One- or two-bedroom condos wouldn't work for them. The city spent millions of dollars building the wrong product for the outcome they wanted.

Sadly, the city of Portland is not the only organization to make this mistake. Every product team has, at one time or another, found themselves facing the hard reality that they spent time, energy, and money building the wrong product. Why does this happen? This chapter will explore why so many teams find themselves in this situation and provide a reliable process for reducing the chance that it will happen to you.

Be Prepared to Be Wrong

Daniel Kahneman, in *Thinking, Fast and Slow*, introduced us to the idea of cognitive biases—mental shortcuts that, while often helpful, sometimes get us into trouble. In the Portland affordable-housing story (and in many others like it), we are seeing an interplay of two cognitive biases—confirmation bias and the escalation of commitment. *Confirmation bias*[45] means we are more likely to seek out confirming evidence than we are to seek out disconfirming evidence. We pay attention to and remember the data that supports our perspective and often ignore or forget the data that undermines our perspective. Both the city and the developer were excited by the positive feedback they got on their project but overlooked the negative feedback. The *escalation of commitment*[46] is a bias in which the more we invest in an idea, the more committed we become to that idea. The more the city explored this idea (and this idea alone), the more committed to the idea they became—despite its flaws.

Product teams are particularly susceptible to confirmation bias and the escalation of commitment. We tend to fall in love with our ideas. We often have to defend our ideas to stakeholders, further entrenching our commitment to our ideas. We tend to seek out why our ideas will work and forget to explore why they might *not* work. As a result, we are often overconfident about the success of our ideas.

Chip and Dan Heath, authors of *Decisive* (introduced in Chapter 2), advise that, if we want to avoid overconfidence and make better decisions, we need to be prepared to be wrong. You've already learned some techniques to help you adopt a "prepare to be wrong" mindset. In Chapter 7, you learned to compare and contrast opportunities, so that you aren't overcommitting to one. In Chapter 8, you whittled your ideas down to three, again so that you don't overcommit to one. In this and the next chapter, we'll explore how working with a set of ideas (that all have the potential

---

45 Daniel Kahneman discusses confirmation bias and many other cognitive biases in his book *Thinking, Fast and Slow*. Chip and Dan Heath also dive into confirmation bias in *Decisive*.
46 Robert Cialdini has a great explanation of the escalation of commitment in his book *Influence*.

to solve the same target opportunity) will help us compare and contrast the ideas against each other, helping us to avoid confirmation bias and the escalation of commitment.

However, the way most teams test ideas isn't feasible when working with a set of ideas. We can't build three ideas for the same target opportunity and A/B test them to see which is the most effective. It would take too long. More often than not, designing and building a testable prototype of each idea will take more time than we have. Instead, we need to learn how to quickly test our ideas through fast iterations.

In the opening quote of this chapter, Marty Cagan, author of *INSPIRED*, highlights that the best product teams complete a dozen or more discovery iterations every week. This pace is possible only when we step away from the concept of testing ideas and instead focus on testing the assumptions that need to be true in order for our ideas to succeed. By explicitly enumerating our assumptions, we can start to look for both confirming and disconfirming evidence to either support or refute each assumption. Additionally, assumption testing is generally quicker than idea testing, and the faster pace helps us to guard against the escalation of commitment. The less time we invest in an idea, the less likely we are to fall in love with it.

The biggest barrier to testing assumptions is becoming aware of the assumptions we are making. This chapter will enumerate several strategies for helping you to identify the hidden assumptions behind your solution ideas.

Types of Assumptions

Assumptions come in all shapes and sizes. As product trios, we are primarily concerned with assumptions in the following categories:[17]

Desirability assumptions: Does anyone want it? Will our customers get value from it? As we create solutions, we assume that our customers will want to use our solution, that they will be willing to do the things that we need them to do, and that they'll trust us to provide those solutions. All of these types of assumptions fall into the desirability category.

Viability assumptions: Should we build it? There are many ideas that will work for our customers but won't work for our business. If we want to continue to serve customers over time, we need to make sure that our solutions are viable—that they create a return for our business. This typically means that the idea will generate more revenue than it will cost to build, service, and maintain. However, some ideas are designed to be loss leaders and instead contribute to another business goal besides revenue. But somewhere down the line, the idea must create enough value for the business to be worth the effort to create and maintain.

Feasibility assumptions: Can we build it? We primarily think about feasibility as technical feasibility. Is it technically possible? Feasibility assumptions, however, can also include, "What's feasible

---

47   The idea that a successful product is viable, feasible, and desirable has been around for years in the product industry. In trying to track down the origin, many people referred me to the IDEO Human Centered Design Toolkit. However, it may have been used even earlier by Anthony Ulwick, when he introduced the "Jobs to be Done" framework.

for our business?" For example, will our legal or security team allow for it? Will our culture support it? Does it comply with regulations?[48]

Usability assumptions: Is it usable? Can customers find what they need? Will they understand how to use it or what they need to do? Are they able to do what we need them to do? Is it accessible?

Ethical assumptions: Is there any potential harm in building this idea? This is an area that is grossly underdeveloped for many product trios. As an industry, we need to do a better job of asking questions like: What data are we collecting? How are we storing it? How are we using it? If our customers had full transparency to those answers, would they be okay with it?

But this category isn't limited to data usage. While some products or services have clear potential harm—think autonomous vehicles—even more pedestrian products have the potential for harm. Reading the news has the potential to change our mood or disrupt our day. Facebook has the potential to inspire FOMO, imposter syndrome, or a feeling of falling behind our peers, not to mention it's habit-forming in a way that may be detrimental to our well-being. Every product introduces some potential for harm. As product trios, we don't always need to mitigate every potential area for harm, but we should be aware of the impact our products and services are having and ask how we can reduce the potential harm.

Story Map to Get Clarity

It's hard to enumerate our assumptions if we aren't specific about what our ideas mean. After ideating, our ideas tend to be vague concepts. You can fit only so many words on a sticky note (virtual or physical). Even if you've taken the time to describe

---

48 Some thought leaders consider feasibility as technical feasibility alone and categorize legal, security, and compliance concerns as viability assumptions. To me, they make more sense as feasibility assumptions. But how we categorize them doesn't really matter. What matters is that we enumerate them, question them, and, when needed, test them.

your ideas, odds are each person in your trio is interpreting the idea differently. This means that each person is making their own assumptions about how the idea will work. It's hard to test your underlying assumptions when you don't yet agree on what those assumptions are.

One of the best ways to align as a team around what your ideas mean is to story map them. Story mapping is a popular technique in which teams map out each step end-users have to take to get value from a product or service.[49] Story mapping forces you to get specific about how an idea will work and what you expect your end-users will do. While many teams use story mapping to align around product requirements, it's also a great technique for helping us to surface underlying assumptions.

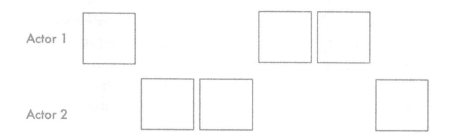

To story map your ideas:

Start by assuming the solution already exists. You aren't story mapping what it will take to implement an idea. Instead, you are mapping what end-users will do to get value from the solution once it exists in the world.

Identify the key actors. Who needs to interact with whom for the idea to work? Some products like Slack or Facebook require that two or more end-users interact with each other for anyone to get value from the product. If this is the case, you'll want to represent multiple end-users in your story map. In two-sided marketplaces,

---

49 If you are new to story mapping, see Jeff Patton's book *User Story Mapping*.

you might have different types of end-users (e.g., buyers and sellers). In some products or services, the interface or software itself may be an actor in your map (e.g., for an end-user conversing with a chatbot, the chatbot should be listed as a player in the story map).

Map out the steps each actor has to take for anyone to get value from the solution. Be specific. What does each actor need to do in order for someone to get value from the solution? For example, an actor has to engage with a chatbot by asking a question or making a request, the chatbot then needs to respond, and so on.

Sequence the steps horizontally over time. Lay out the steps horizontally one after the other. Sequence them in the order they need to happen. You may need to jump back and forth between players if they need to take turns taking actions. It's okay if some steps are optional. List them in the map where they might occur. If an end-user can choose multiple paths, map out the successful path. If there are multiple successful paths, map them out sequentially.

Let's walk through an example. Suppose we are working at our streaming-entertainment company, and we are exploring three different solutions (setting up a good compare-and-contrast decision) for the target opportunity "I want to watch live sports."

1. Integrate local networks (e.g., ABC, CBS, NBC) into our service
2. License broadcast rights directly from the different sports leagues and serve the sporting events up ourselves
3. Bundle our streaming service with a partner who streams live sports

To story map our first idea—integrating local networks—we need to start by identifying the key players. In this case, it's easy to make the mistake of thinking our key players are our business-development folks and their equivalent at the respective local channel providers. But remember, with story mapping, we want to assume the solution already exists. We aren't story mapping what it would take to build the service—we are story mapping what the key players need to do for our consumer to get value from it.

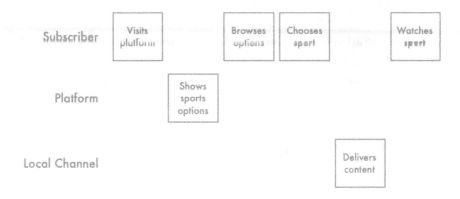

So, in this case, our key players might be the sports consumer (i.e., our subscriber), our streaming platform, and any number of local TV channel partners. Our story map might include the following steps:

- Our subscriber comes to our platform to watch live sports.
- Our platform has live sports options for our subscriber to choose from.
- Our subscriber browses the options and chooses a sport that is currently on a local TV channel.
- Our local channel provider's content is available to stream.
- Our subscriber watches live sports.

Now, even though this story map is quite simple, we may still need to make some critical decisions along the way. Can we offer the ability to search for a specific sport or a specific sporting event on our platform? In other words, can the local provider share their listings with us in a format that we can integrate into our own search results? Or does the subscriber need to know the game they want to watch is on NBC and they need to search for NBC? We don't have to know all the answers right now.

Instead, we want to story map what we think would be the best solution based on what we know today. You can see that, in the above map, we assumed that the sports search would happen on the streaming-entertainment platform. We are assuming that's possible. That's okay. We have to make assumptions before we can test assumptions. But don't worry about whether you are getting everything exactly right. We'll have plenty of time to iterate and refine our ideas as we test our assumptions. This is merely a starting point.

Use Your Story Maps to Generate Assumptions

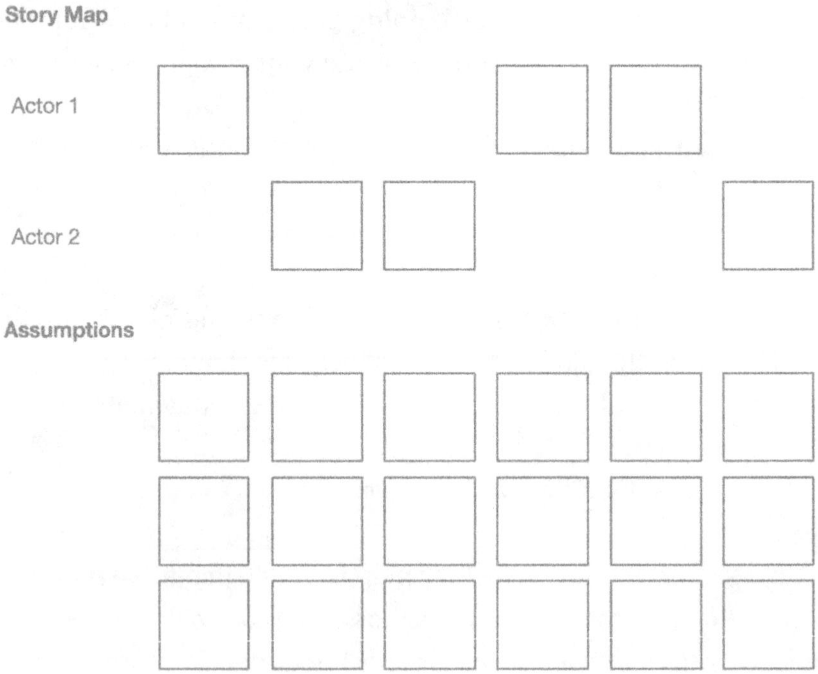

Story Map

Actor 1

Actor 2

Assumptions

Now that your product trio has a clear concept of what your idea means, you can use your story map to uncover hidden assumptions.

Throughout your story map, every time you assume that an end-user will do something, you are making desirability assumptions (i.e., that your user wants to do what you are asking them to do and that they are willing to do it), usability assumptions (i.e., your user understands what needs to be done and is able to do it), and feasibility assumptions (i.e., you can build whatever is required to support each step of the map). You can literally go step by step through your story map and generate dozens of assumptions.

Let's return to our example to see how this works. From our first step of the story map, "Our subscriber comes to our platform to watch sports," we can generate the following assumptions:

- Desirability: Our subscriber wants to watch sports.
- Desirability: Our subscriber wants to watch sports on our platform.
- Usability: Our subscriber knows they can watch sports on our platform.
- Usability: Our subscriber thinks of our platform when it's time to watch sports.
- Feasibility: Our platform is available when our subscriber wants to watch sports.

From our second step, "Our platform has live sports options for our subscriber to choose from," we can generate the following assumptions:

- Desirability: Our platform has the sports our subscriber wants to watch.
- Usability: Our subscriber can find where to go on our platform to find sports.
- Feasibility: We know what sports are available right now.
- Feasibility: We can display what sports are available right now.

From our third step, "Our subscriber chooses a sport that is currently on a local TV channel," we can generate the following assumptions:

- Desirability: Our subscriber wants to watch a sport that is on a local TV channel.
- Usability: Our subscriber can find the sport they want to watch.
- Usability: Our subscriber knows how to select and play the sport they want to watch.

From our fourth step, "Our local channel provider's content is available," we can generate the following assumptions:

- Feasibility: The local provider's source content will be available.
- Feasibility: We can display the content from our local provider.
- Desirability: The content we display is what the consumer wanted.

From our fourth step, "Our subscriber watches live sports," we can generate the following assumptions:

- Desirability: The subscriber likes what they chose.
- Feasibility: The stream works well enough for the subscriber to enjoy live sports.
- Usability: The interface doesn't detract from watching the sport.

Sometimes story maps can help us uncover viability and ethical assumptions as well. For example, this story map might help us realize that we are making the following viability and ethical assumptions:

- Viability: Integrating a local channel feed won't be too expensive.
- Ethical: Subscribers will be okay with us sharing viewership data with their local channels.

However, you'll learn more specific techniques for highlighting viability and ethical assumptions in the coming sections.

From a simple 5-step story map, we generated 20 assumptions.

Now if you are feeling overwhelmed, don't worry. Assumptions aren't bad. If we've done our discovery homework (e.g., continuous interviewing, opportunity mapping, etc.), we'll understand our customers' context well, and most of our assumptions will be true enough. You'll see, later in this chapter, that we won't even bother testing most of them. However, by taking the time to generate many assumptions, we'll increase the likelihood that we'll uncover the risky ones. Later in this chapter, you'll learn how to prioritize and identify the riskiest assumptions.

Conduct a Pre-Mortem

Story maps aren't the only way to help us see our own assumptions. Gary Klein, a cognitive psychologist and author of several books on decision-making, flipped the idea of a post-mortem on its head. Post-mortems are after-project reviews where participants assess what went wrong and what could have gone better. Sprint retrospectives are a type of post-mortem. Pre-mortems, on the other hand, happen at the start of the project and are designed to suss out what could go wrong in the future.

Pre-mortems are a great way to generate assumptions. They leverage prospective hindsight—a technique where you imagine what might happen in the future. A pre-mortem encourages you to ask, "Imagine it's six months in the future; your product or initiative launched, and it was a complete failure. What went wrong?"

As you generate reasons for why your product or service might fail, you are exposing assumptions that your idea depends upon that may not be true.

The success of pre-mortems, however, hinges on one key factor—phrasing the question as if the outcome is certain. In our case, that means we have to consider that the product or service *did* fail, not that it *might* fail. Deborah Mitchell, Edward Russo, and Nancy Pennington, collaborating psychologists at the University of Pennsylvania, Cornell University, and the University of Colorado, found the technique was effective at generating better explanations only when prospective hindsight was paired with a certain outcome.[50]

Walk the Lines of Your Opportunity Solution Tree

Another way to generate assumptions, particularly viability assumptions, is to use your opportunity solution tree to work backwards from your solution back to your outcome. You can start by generating assumptions using the following starters:

- This solution will address the target opportunity because…
- Addressing the target opportunity will drive the desired outcome because…

Be specific. Why will your solution address the target opportunity? Your answer will contain one or more assumptions that you'll want to capture. For example, "Adding local channels will allow our subscribers to watch live sports" because "The sports that our subscribers want to watch are on local channels" because "Most of

---

50 Mitchell, Deborah, Russo, J., and Pennington, Nancy. (1989). "Back to the future: Temporal perspective in the explanation of events." *Journal of Behavioral Decision-Making*. 2. 25–38. 10.1002/bdm.3960020103.

the major sports are on local channels" and "Our subscribers are more likely to want to watch major sports." Each phrase in quotes is an assumption we can test.

Why does addressing the opportunity "I want to watch live sports" drive the outcome "Increase weekly viewer minutes"? "People will watch sports in addition to what they already watch." "Even if people cut out other shows, sporting events are long, and their individual viewing sessions will be longer." "If individual viewing sessions are longer, weekly viewing minutes will go up."

Now if our desired outcome is a product outcome (as it should be), we might also need to test the assumptions connecting our product outcome to our business outcome to uncover viability assumptions. "People who watch more minutes are more likely to renew." "The cost of adding local channels will be offset by the gain from more renewals."

The goal is to capture the logical inferences behind why you think this solution will address your target opportunity in a way that drives your product outcomes and ultimately, your business outcome. Each inference is an assumption that you can test.

Explore Potential Harm

One area that product teams often overlook is ethical assumptions. Now, if you work at a nuclear power plant or on autonomous vehicles, safety is probably a daily conversation. But for the rest of us, it's an easy factor to forget. To uncover ethical assumptions, I encourage teams to ask, "What's the potential harm in offering this solution?"

Some teams struggle to come up with anything. But all products have some potential harm. Many products run into ethical dilemmas around their data practices. Here are some questions to ask:

- What data do you plan to collect?

- Do your customers understand that you'll be collecting that data?
- Do your customers understand how you'll be using that data?
- Are you planning to share that data with third parties?
- If yes, how are those third parties planning to use that data?
- If your customers fully understood how you planned to use their data, would they be okay with it?

But ethical assumptions aren't limited to how we use data. We might ask:

- Does our product have the potential to become addictive? Many product teams consider this a good thing. But is it good for your end-user?
- Are there people who are being left out? Are you designing for one demographic and leaving out an under-represented population?
- Are you assuming that your end-users have money, free time, a roof over their head, access to the internet? If so, who does this leave out? What are the implications of that?
- Does this solution contribute to society's inequalities? Or does it help to mitigate the inequalities?
- Are we exposing someone's identity who might need anonymity for their own safety?
- Is there a potential to harm relationships between our end-users?
- How might Internet trolls abuse this?[51]

---

51 See: https://www.mindtheproduct.com/an-ethical-sanity-check-what-would-trolls-do/

Some solutions can cause harm to our business. We might consider:

- Will this solution help or hurt our brand?
- Can we meet customers' expectations, or will we leave them disappointed?
- Are we spending time building the wrong stuff, therefore losing out on more compelling opportunities?

One of my favorite questions to ask teams is, "If the *New York Times/Wall Street Journal/BBC* (or insert your favorite news organization) ran a front-page story about this solution that included your internal conversations about how the solution would work, what data you collected, how you used it, and how different players in the ecosystem benefited or didn't, would that be a good thing? If not, why not?" This is a great way to uncover ethical assumptions.

Mix and Match the Methods

Whenever I reconnect with teams that I've coached in the past, I always like to ask them about their discovery process. Many are embarrassed to say they are no longer story mapping or they no longer walk the lines of their opportunity solution tree. When I ask, "How come?" they always explain they are getting so good at seeing their own assumptions that they don't need to do these steps anymore. There's nothing wrong with that. All of the habits in this book are designed to get you to a specific outcome. This chapter is about helping you become aware of the assumptions you are making and encourages you to explicitly enumerate them.

If you have no idea how to do that, story mapping, pre-mortems, walking the lines of your opportunity solution tree, and questioning potential harm will help you start to see your own assumptions. However, as you exercise this muscle, these methods may become less necessary. That's not a bad thing. That means you are developing your skills around questioning your assumptions.

You don't need to use every method for every idea every time. If you are struggling to enumerate viability assumptions, walk the lines of your opportunity solution tree. If you are great at identifying feasibility assumptions but often forget about desirability assumptions, take some time to story map the idea. Use the methods that shore up your weak spots.

In my experience, most teams have a bias toward one category or another. They are great at testing usability but forget about desirability. Or they always remember desirability and usability, but they forget viability. Most product teams have a blind spot for ethical assumptions. Our intentions are good, so we forget that our product has potential harm. Use the methods that help you address your team's specific blind spots.

Prioritizing Assumptions

Armed with a long list of assumptions for each idea, it's now time to assess and prioritize which assumptions need further testing. Assumption mapping, an exercise designed by David J. Bland, author of *Testing Business Ideas*, is a great way to quickly identify what Bland calls your "leap of faith" assumptions—the assumptions that carry the most risk and thus need to be tested.

With assumption mapping, you'll be quickly evaluating each assumption on two dimensions. I recommend you start with assessing "How much do we know about this assumption?" In other words, what evidence do we already have that tells us this assumption is true or false? If we have a lot of evidence that it's true, then we would place the assumption on the left side of the x-axis. If we have very little evidence, we would place it on the right side of the x-axis.

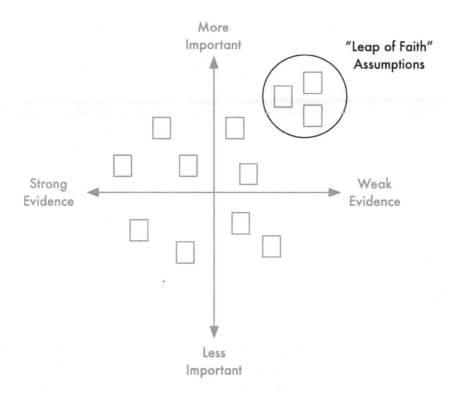

Next, we want to assess how important this assumption is to the success of your idea. Now, all assumptions are important to the success of your idea as currently designed. However, some assumptions can be easily worked around if they turn out not to be true. Others may be much harder to work around. These would make these assumptions more important. The more important an assumption is, the higher on the y-axis it gets placed. The less important it is, the lower on the y-axis it gets placed.

Each assumption lives in one spot on the two-dimensional grid. You want to find the moment in space that represents how important an assumption is to the success of the idea and how much evidence we have or don't have to support it. However, this exercise does not need to be precise. You are mapping assumptions relative to each other. For example, once you place the first assumption, for the second assumption, you can now ask, "Do we have stronger or weaker evidence for this assumption as compared to the first assumption, and is this assumption more or less important than the first assumption?" and place it relative to the first assumption.

In my experience running this exercise in workshops and with the teams that I coach, teams do just as well when they do this exercise fast (i.e., no more than ten minutes per idea) as when they deliberate and discuss every placement. So, save yourself some time, and go fast.

Additionally, some teams have a bias toward everything being important and having weak evidence. That's okay. All of your assumptions have some degree of both. Whether your assumptions are all jammed in the upper-right corner or are spread across all four quadrants, it doesn't matter. What does matter is that your assumptions are positioned relative to each other.

Once we've completed our mapping, we are going to start by testing the assumptions in the top-most, right-most corner. Bear in mind, this does not mean you are testing all of the assumptions in the top-right quadrant. We often don't have time for that. It means you are starting with the two or three assumptions that fall in the upper-right corner. Those are your most important assumptions with the weakest evidence—the assumptions that Bland calls your "leap of faith" assumptions.

You'll want to story map, generate assumptions, and assumption map for each of your three ideas. In the next chapter, we'll learn how to quickly test your "leap of faith" assumptions for each of your ideas so that you are able to compare and contrast the ideas against each other.

Avoid These Common Anti-Patterns

As you work to identify the hidden assumptions behind your ideas, be sure to avoid these common anti-patterns:

Not generating enough assumptions. Generating assumptions, like ideating, is intended to be a divergent exercise. The goal is to identify as many "gotchas" as you can to increase the chance that you generate the riskiest ones. However, many teams dramatically underestimate how many assumptions underlie their ideas. When I do these exercises, I often generate 20–30 assumptions for even a simple idea. If that sounds overwhelming, remember, you won't need to test all of these assumptions. Most of them will be harmless. You'll use the assumption-mapping exercise to quickly find the riskiest ones. However, if you don't generate the riskiest assumptions, the mapping exercise won't help you sort something that you haven't uncovered. Use the five assumption categories and the exercises in this chapter to help you generate as many assumptions as you can.

Phrasing your assumptions such that you need them to be false. Generating assumptions can be a bit of a devil's-advocate exercise. You are looking for what might go wrong with your ideas. As a result, you might be tempted to phrase your assumptions negatively. For example, if you need your users to log in to your service, you might phrase your assumption as, "Customers won't remember their password." However, this is backwards. You need customers to remember their password for your idea to work. When you are generating assumptions, always phrase your assumptions such that you need them to be true: "Customers will remember their passwords." For many assumptions, you'll find that this positive framing will make them easier to test.

Not being specific enough. I see many teams generate assumptions like this: "Customers will have time," "Customers will know what to do," and "Our engineers can build something like this." These assumptions are not specific enough to test. What will customers have time for? What do you need them to know how to do? What do engineers need to build? Be specific. These assumptions are much better: "Customers will take the time to browse all the options on our getting-started page," "Customers will know how to select the right option based on their situation," and "Our engineers can identify the right subset of options to show the customer based on the customer's profile data."

Favoring one category at the cost of other categories. Most teams have a bias toward one or two categories at the cost of the other categories. Some teams conflate desirability and usability and forget that just because a product is usable doesn't mean it's desirable. For products with challenging feasibility issues, it can be hard to remember to first test and see if customers even want the solution. Most teams forget about ethical assumptions altogether. Remember: Use the categories to catch your blind spots.

CHAPTER TEN

TESTING ASSUMPTIONS, NOT IDEAS

"Good tests kill flawed theories; we remain alive to guess again."
— Karl Popper

*"Each answer a team collects—positive or
negative—is a unit of progress"*
— Jeff Gothelf and Josh Seiden, *Sense & Respond*

Armed with your "leap of faith" assumptions for three ideas, you might be tempted to rush into assumption testing. It's exhilarating to get an experiment live and start collecting data. In my coaching program, teams learn to identify assumptions one week and then learn to test assumptions in the following week. Sometimes teams get so excited about testing assumptions that they come to their session during the identifying-assumptions week and report that they've already started collecting data on some of their top assumptions.

I admire these teams' bias toward action. But more often than not, we find problems with their assumption tests. Sometimes their tests aren't designed to test their "leap of faith" assumption but instead are designed to test the whole idea. Even after doing all the work to identify our riskiest assumptions, it's easy to get distracted by our great ideas. Sometimes the team hasn't agreed on what success looks like upfront, and they aren't sure how to interpret their results. Sometimes they test with the wrong audience, or they get distracted by interesting, but not meaningful, data. These teams are all smart, capable, motivated product trios. However, it's easy to rush into experimenting before we are ready.

When we rush our experiments, we tend to throw spaghetti at the wall, hoping something sticks. We try variations with abandon, instead of systematically searching for our best option. We run countless tests with little impact. We forget to clearly define what we are trying to learn and what success looks like, leaving us with ambiguous results.

If you've ever run an experiment and weren't sure how to interpret the results, or if you've ever wondered if your prototype feedback was good enough, this chapter is for you. You'll learn how to slow down (just a little bit) to make sure you get more value from each and every assumption test.

Working With Sets of Ideas

As we start assumption testing, we want to make sure that we carry forward the idea of comparing and contrasting our ideas against each other. It's easy to overcommit to our favorite idea. Why do the work to test three ideas when the best idea looks so good? This is where we want to take a minute to remind ourselves of the cognitive biases we discussed in the previous chapter—confirmation bias and the escalation of commitment.

If we test only one idea at a time, confirmation bias will rear its ugly head. We'll be more likely to notice the confirming evidence and miss the disconfirming evidence. Similarly, the more time we invest in a single idea, thanks to the escalation of commitment, the more likely we'll be all-in, committing to the idea, even if it has flaws.

Instead, we want to systematically collect evidence about our assumptions underlying all three ideas. The more we learn about each idea, the more likely we are to compare and contrast the ideas against each other. This helps us make better decisions about which ideas are most promising. Remember—we are looking for a clear front runner.

As you read through the rest of this chapter, remember: We aren't testing one idea at a time. We are testing assumptions from a set of ideas.

Simulate an Experience, Evaluate Behavior

With assumption testing, our goal is to collect data that will help us move the assumption from the right to the left on our assumption map (see Chapter 9)—we are starting with an assumption that has weak supporting evidence, and our goal is to collect more evidence. Just like with interviewing (see Chapter 5), to collect reliable data, we want to focus on collecting data about what people actually do in a particular context, not just what they think or say they do in general.

A strong assumption test simulates an experience, giving your participant the opportunity to behave either in accordance with your assumption or not. This behavior is what allows us to evaluate our assumption.

To construct a good assumption test, you'll want to think carefully about the right moment to simulate. You don't want to simulate any more than you need to. This is what allows you to iterate quickly through several assumption tests.

Let's return to our streaming-entertainment example, where we are trying to address the target opportunity "I want to watch sports" and we've brainstormed a set of solutions—adding local channels, licensing events directly from sports leagues, and bundling our service with a sports provider.

If we are testing the assumption, "Our subscribers want to watch sports," we might simulate the moment when someone is browsing their streaming options, trying to decide what to watch. We could do this by mocking up the "home screen" that users see when they turn on the streaming-entertainment service. We could present them with several options, including a handful of sporting events, popular TV shows, and recent movie releases. We could then ask them, "What would you prefer to watch right now?"

If we are trying to test the assumption "Our subscriber wants to watch sports on our platform," we might simulate the moment in time when the big game is about to start. Since our platform doesn't currently offer sports, we can't simply ask them which service they prefer. Instead, we might present them with three subscription services (including ours), tell them that the game is available on all three services, and ask them to choose a service to stream the game.

Now, neither of these simulations is perfect. What I say I want to watch when talking to a stranger might differ from what I want to watch when I'm at home by myself. Or I might favor one subscription on one day and another subscription on another day. That's okay. Perfect simulations are hard to come by. Instead, we'll account for these shortcomings when we decide how to evaluate the results of our simulation.

Notice how all three ideas depend on the assumption "Our subscriber wants to watch sports." This is an assumption that is core to the target opportunity, so if this assumption is false, we can abandon our set of ideas. However, only the first and second ideas depend on the assumption "Our subscribers want to watch sports on our platform." It's common for ideas to share assumptions. It's one of the reasons why assumption testing is faster than idea testing. Assumption tests don't merely give us a go/no-go decision for an individual idea; they help us evaluate sets of ideas. We'll also see later how shared assumptions will help us generate even better ideas after a round or two of testing.

Once we've identified the moment in time that we want to simulate, we now need to define how we'll evaluate the behavior we observe. Our goal when considering our simulation evaluation is to define what success looks like. In other words, if our assumption is true, what would we expect the participant to do?

For example, when observing people selecting what to watch, we might evaluate how many people choose to watch a sporting event vs. how many people don't. If our assumption is true—that our subscribers do want to watch sports—we would expect at least some of them to choose a sporting event in our simulation.

When simulating the moment before the big game starts, we might want to evaluate how many people think of our platform as the place to watch the game vs. another platform. If our assumption is true—that our subscribers did want to watch sports on our platform—then we would expect some of them to choose our service over the competitors'.

Now, in both simulations, we say "some people" should exhibit the behavior we expect. The problem with "some" is that your product manager might define "some" as 5 out of 10, and your designer might define "some" as 20 out of 100.

If you run your simulation with 10 people, and 6 people choose sports, your product manager is going to think your assumption is now more known, and your designer is still going to be skeptical. The challenge with this scenario is that, as a team, you didn't learn anything new from this assumption test because you disagree on what the results mean.

To avoid this situation, we want to get specific with our evaluation criteria. Instead of saying, "Some people choose sports," we want to say, "At least 3 out of 10 people choose sports." We want to define both how many people we'll test with and how many people need to exhibit the behavior that we expect to see.

By defining these criteria upfront, you are doing two things. First, you are aligning as a team around what success looks like so that you all know how to interpret the results. This will help to ensure that your assumption tests are actionable. And second, you are helping to guard against confirmation bias. Remember, confirmation bias makes us more likely to see the evidence that our idea will succeed than the evidence that it might not succeed. If we don't define our success criteria upfront, when we try to interpret the results, our brains will actively look for evidence that supports the assumption, and we'll likely miss the evidence that could refute it. To avoid this, we want to define what success looks like upfront (before we see the results).

So how do we choose the numbers? This is a subjective decision. Your goal is to find the right balance between speed of testing and what aligns your team around an actionable outcome. You want to test your assumption with as few people as possible (as it will be faster) but with the number of people that still gives your team the information they need to act on the data. Now remember, you aren't trying to prove that this assumption is true. The burden of truth is too much. You are simply trying to reduce risk. Keep your assumption map in mind. Your goal is to move the assumption from right to left. How many people would convince you this assumption is more known? That's the negotiation you are having as a team.

If your simulation is less than optimal, as we saw with the above examples, you'll need to modify your numbers to accommodate for these shortcomings. If someone raises the concern that some sports fans might want to watch sports on our platform, but in the moment we ask them, they might be more likely to choose a comedy, then you might lower your threshold for success to account for that. If someone else is worried that choosing from three subscriptions biases the results in favor of your subscription (because the reality is people have, on average, five subscription services), then you could either decide to change your mockup to show five services or raise your threshold for your success criteria.

The key outcome with this exercise is to agree as a team on the smallest assumption test you can design that still gets you results that the team will feel comfortable acting on.

Early Signals vs. Large-Scale Experiments

Inevitably, someone on your team is going to raise a concern with making decisions based on small numbers. How can we have confidence in the data if we talk to only five customers? You might be tempted to test with larger pools of people to help get buy-in. But this strategy comes at a cost—it takes more time. We don't want to invest the time, energy, and effort into an experiment if we don't even have an early signal that we are on the right track.

Rather than starting with a large-scale experiment (e.g., surveying hundreds of customers, launching a production-quality A/B test, worrying about representative samples), we want to start small. You'll be pleasantly surprised by how much you can learn from getting feedback from a handful of customers.

Imagine we test the assumption, "Our subscribers want to watch sports," as described above. We show participants a mockup of our "home screen," and we ask them what they'd like to watch. Four out of ten choose a sporting event, soaring past the threshold we set for our success criteria. What will we do next?

It depends. We've made this assumption more known. However, we can't conclude it's true. It still carries risk. The question becomes, "How much risk?" If we have another assumption on our assumption map that is now riskier, we want to switch gears and test that assumption. But if this assumption continues to be our riskiest assumption, and it carries more risk than our organization can stomach, then we need to continue to test it. We need to start defining the next-level experiment that will allow us to collect more data.

Perhaps, as a next step, we decide to add a section to our real "home screen" promoting an upcoming sporting event. When users select it, it informs them that we are considering adding sports to our lineup, and we ask for feedback by way of a thumbs-up or a thumbs-down. We also give them the option to submit comments. We think we can get this experiment live with a week of development work. We decide to collect data from 500 participants (which we think we can do in 3 days), and we set our success criteria to at least 100 of the 500 participants giving us a thumbs-up. This is a classic smoke-screen test.

So why didn't we start here? Our first test was designed to be completed in a day or two. This test will take up to two weeks—maybe longer, if we need to get permission from stakeholders and/or need to wait for an upcoming release cycle. We don't want to invest this time, energy, and effort until we've received an early signal that we are on the right track.

With assumption testing, most of our learning comes from failed tests. That's when we learn that something we thought was true might not be. Small tests give us a chance to fail sooner. Failing faster is what allows us to quickly move on to the next assumption, idea, or opportunity. Karl Popper, a renowned 20th-century philosopher of science, in the opening quote argues, "Good tests kill flawed theories," preventing us from investing where there is little reward, and "we remain alive to guess again," giving us another chance to get it right.

As we test assumptions, we want to start small and iterate our way to bigger, more reliable, more sound tests, only after each previous round provides an indicator that continuing to invest is worth our effort. We stop testing when we've removed enough risk and/or the effort to run the next test is so great that it makes more sense to simply build the idea.

Understanding False Positives and False Negatives

Now, this method isn't flawless. When working with small numbers, we will encounter false positives and false negatives. Let's explore the impact of these errors on our work.

In your first round of experimenting, it is possible that you'll select 10 participants who all hate sports. We can mitigate the risk of this by choosing a variety of folks. In other words, we don't want to choose 10 participants from Honolulu, Hawaii (where no major sports teams reside), and expect to get reliable results. Instead, we want to select for variation in geographic location, demographics, TV-watching behavior, etc., as best we can. However, even if we select for variation, it is still possible that none of our participants like sports when our larger population does. That's because we aren't doing the work to select a representative sample, and we aren't testing with large-enough numbers.

When this happens, when our experiment fails, even though our larger population exhibits the behavior that we want to see, we call this a "false negative." Our test is providing data that indicates our assumption is faulty when it may not be.

But what's the cost of this false negative? In this particular example, where our assumption is testing our target opportunity "Our subscribers want to watch sports," we might consider abandoning the opportunity. However, we aren't likely to make this decision based on one failed test. Instead, if we are running tests across our set of ideas, we will have additional data points to help us evaluate the target opportunity.

For example, if we test assumptions across three different ideas, all exploring if our subscribers are interested in sports, and all of them fail, then the chance that all of them are false negatives goes down. More likely, we'll get conflicting results. We'll see one assumption fail and another one pass. We'll need to dig in to learn why. In the worst-case scenario, one of our results will be a false negative, and we'll have to run additional experiments to evaluate our assumption. However, if our tests are small, this costs us only a day or two. This isn't a very costly false negative.

Most of our assumptions, however, aren't testing the opportunity. They are testing some aspect of a particular solution. When these assumptions fail, we typically design around them. We evolve our ideas so that they no longer depend on the faulty assumption. For example, if we are testing the assumption "Our subscribers know where to find sports on our platform," and it turns out to be problematic, we can always redesign the interface to make sports easier to find. If our failure was a false negative, it's possible we might redesign our interface when we don't need to. But if further testing shows that our iteration works, the cost of this false negative is only the time it took to do the redesign. Again, this false negative isn't that costly, as long as we keep our iterations and our future testing small.

Additionally, when we run fast iterations, we are in a better position to make decisions using multiple data points from several tests rather than make decisions based on a single data point. We can test if our subscribers want to watch sports through a number of testing methods. We can ask them about their past viewing behavior and see if they have watched sports in the past. We can show them a mockup and ask them what they would like to watch right now. We can simulate the moment before the big game and see if they choose our service. Instead of throwing out an assumption based on one data point, we can draw conclusions from the set of assumption tests. Researchers call this triangulation.[52] It's using a mix of research methods to better understand the assumption we are testing.

Finally, even in the worst-case scenario, when we do decide to abandon an idea or an opportunity and it turns out it was based on

---

52   See: https://ebn.bmj.com/content/22/3/67

a false negative, it's still okay. There are hundreds, if not thousands, of ideas that could address our target opportunity or opportunities that could drive our desired outcome. When we throw one away needlessly, it's not that costly, as long as we find an idea that does work or an opportunity that does have an impact. Remember, there isn't one right idea or one right opportunity. We can afford false negatives because ideas and opportunities are abundant.

Now let's turn to false positives. A false positive is when our test gives us data suggesting that our assumption is true, when it isn't. This sounds far riskier than a false negative, but, in practice, it's not. Suppose we run our small test, and we learn that everyone wants to watch sports, so we call our test a success, and we move forward. Remember, we aren't making a go/no-go decision based on one assumption test. We are either moving on to test another assumption related to the same idea, or we are running a bigger, more reliable test on the same assumption. If our idea really is faulty, odds are that our next round of assumption testing will catch it. False positives usually get surfaced in successive rounds of testing. The cost of a false positive in a small test is usually the time and effort required to run the next-bigger test. That's not trivial, but we still avoid the far-bigger cost of building the wrong solutions.

I want to be clear: There is a cost to false negatives and false positives. And we should be aware that these costs exist. But the cost is not so great that we should be starting with large-scale, quantitative experiments every time. If we did that, we would never ship any software. Our tests would simply take too long. The vast majority of the time, you will learn plenty from your small-scale tests.

A Quick Word on Science

Science-minded readers might cringe at these quick-and-dirty research methods. However, product teams are not scientists. Scientists work to understand the fundamental laws of the universe.

They are seeking truths, creating new knowledge. In science (and the rest of academia), truth is determined over decades. Research studies are designed and replicated by a community of scientists. Truth starts to emerge from a meta-analysis of years of research. Even then, our truths don't always stand the test of time. Newton's laws of physics are true in some contexts, but with quantum physics, we are learning there are contexts in which they are not true. Newton's truths are incomplete. In social science, we think a landmark research study means one thing, until years of more research show there was a confounding variable that wasn't accounted for. Social-science truths often evolve. Research is messy, and creating new knowledge is hard.

Product teams, fortunately, are not creating new knowledge. Instead, we are trying to create products that improve our customers' lives. When we launch a new product or service, we get to see how our customers interact with it. This is a fantastic feedback loop. We quickly get to measure if our product had the intended impact. We work on much faster cycles than science. It took almost 100 years before we could collect physical evidence to support Einstein's theory of general relativity.[53]

So, while we want to adopt a scientific mindset and we want to think about the reliability and the validity of the data that we collect, we are not running scientific experiments. While we need to be thoughtful about our research methods, we also need to be aware that we are not validating or invalidating anything. It's important that we recognize that our research findings are not truths—they are merely confirming or disconfirming evidence that either supports or refutes our point of view. Our goal as a product team is not to *seek truth* but to *mitigate risk*. We need to do just enough research to mitigate the risk that our companies cannot bear and no more.

---

53   See: https://www.nytimes.com/2016/02/12/science/ligo-gravitational-waves-black-holes-einstein.html

This understanding of the intent behind our research will help us strike the right balance between sound research methods and the pace at which we need to work to get products into our customers' hands.

Running Assumption Tests

The Identifying Hidden Assumptions chapter (Chapter 9) opened with a quote from Marty Cagan, in which he argued the best teams conduct 15–20 discovery iterations a week. This can sound like an overwhelming number of assumption tests. But with the right mindset, tools, and methods, it can quickly become a reality. In Chapter 9, we learned that the secret to unlocking this cadence is testing assumptions, not whole ideas. However, we still need to learn how to quickly execute our assumption tests.

There are two tools that should be in every product team's toolbox—unmoderated user testing and one-question surveys. Unmoderated user-testing services allow you to post a stimulus (e.g., a prototype) and define tasks to complete and questions to answer. Participants then complete the tasks and answer the questions on their own time. You get a video of their work. These types of tools are game changers. Instead of having to recruit 10 participants and run the sessions yourself, you can post your task, go home for the night, and come back the next day to a set of videos ready for you to watch.

If we look at the two simulations we designed above, both could be conducted with unmoderated testing tools. Once results come in, we would simply have to watch the videos and record how many chose sports in the first assumption test and how many chose our subscription service in the second assumption test. What used to take weeks to recruit, schedule, and conduct a prototype test can now be done in a day or two.

To make unmoderated testing work well, you need to be thoughtful about who you recruit. With both of our tests, we need to recruit our own subscribers. So, we'll need to screen for this. We also want to pay particular attention to variation (as discussed above). This is also something we can screen for. Some unmoderated testing tools also allow you to upload your own list of participants. This is particularly helpful when testing with niche audiences.

Many assumptions can be tested with quick answers to a single question. This is where one-question survey tools can be tremendously helpful. If we wanted to test the "Our subscribers want to watch sports" assumption in more than one way, we could launch a one-question survey asking them, "When was the last time you watched a sporting event?" We could use their answers to triangulate with our prototype simulation.

Sometimes we simply need to learn about our customers' preferences. For example, if we were testing the assumption "Our platform has the sports our subscribers want to watch," we could test this with a one-question survey. We could ask, "Please select all the sports you've watched in the past month."

When using one-question surveys, we want to make sure we are following the same research rules we've outlined before. When asking about past behavior, we want to ask about specific instances (as you learned in Chapter 5). So, we are asking about the last week and the last month, not in general. We also want to avoid asking about what they might do in the future. We know this leads to unreliable data.

Sometimes you can use one-question surveys to simulate an experience. For example, if one of our ideas depends on the assumption "Our subscribers will tell us who their favorite sports teams are," you might be tempted to ask customers, "Are you willing to tell us who your favorite sports teams are?" But this is a question about future behavior. The answers are unreliable. Instead, ask, "What are your favorite sports teams?" Evaluate the results based on the percentage of people who answer as compared to the percentage of people who skipped it.

However, unmoderated testing and one-question surveys aren't the only ways to test assumptions. Sometimes we already have the data we need in our own database. For example, we might look at how many of our current subscribers have searched for sports on our platform and use this as an indicator of interest in sports. Before you dive into the data, be sure to define your evaluation criteria upfront. How many search queries will you sample? How many need to be related to sports? How will you determine "related to sports"? Remember, aligning around success criteria upfront guards against confirmation bias and ensures that your team agrees on what the results mean.

Product teams can typically test most of their assumptions with a combination of prototype tests (either unmoderated or in person), one-question surveys, or through data-mining. However, there are dozens of experiment types. If you want to do a deep dive on qualitative tests, pick up a copy of Laura Klein's *UX for Lean Startups*. She does a good job of surveying a wide breadth of methods. Another great reference is David Bland's *Testing Business Ideas*. The last third of David's book is an encyclopedia of experiment types. However, don't get overwhelmed with having to master all of these experiment types. If you keep the simple assumption-simulate-evaluate framework in mind, you'll be well on your way to becoming a strong assumption tester.

Avoid These Common Anti-Patterns

As you design and run your assumption tests, keep these common anti-patterns in mind:

Overly complex simulations. Some teams spend countless hours, days, or even weeks trying to design and develop the perfect simulation. It's easy to lose sight of the goal. In your first round of testing, you are looking to design fast tests that will help you gather quick signals. Design your tests to be completed in a day or two, or a week, at most. This will ensure that you can keep your discovery iterations high.

Using percentages instead of specific numbers when defining evaluation criteria. Many teams equate 70% and 7 out of 10. So instead of defining their evaluation criteria as 7 out of 10, they tend to favor the percentage. These sound equivalent, but they aren't. First, when testing with small numbers, we can't conclude that 7 out of 10 will continue to mean 70% as our participant size grows. We want to make sure that we don't draw too strong a conclusion from our small signals. Second, and more importantly, "70%" is ambiguous. If we test with 10 people and only 6 exhibit our desired behavior, some of us might conclude that the test failed. Others might argue that we need to test with more people. Be explicit from the get-go about how many people you will test with when defining your success criteria.

Not defining enough evaluation criteria. It's easy to forget important evaluation criteria. At a minimum, you need to define how many people to test with and how many will exhibit the desired behavior. But for some tests, defining the desired behavior may involve more than one number. For example, if your test involves sending an email, you might need to define how many people will receive the email, how long you'll give them to open the email, and whether your success criteria is "opens" or "clicks." Pay particular attention to the success threshold. Complex actions may require multiple measurements (e.g., opens the email, clicks on the link, takes an action).

Testing with the wrong audience. Make sure that you are testing with the right people. If you are testing solutions for a specific target opportunity, make sure that your participants experience the need, pain point, or desire represented by that target opportunity.

Remember to recruit for variation. Don't just test with the easiest audience to reach or the most vocal audience.

Designing for less than the best-case scenario. When testing with small numbers, design your assumption tests such that they are likely to pass. If your assumption test passes with the most likely audience, then you can expand your reach to tougher audiences. This might feel like cheating, but you'll be surprised how often your assumption tests still fail. If you fail in the best-case scenario, your results will be less ambiguous. If your test fails with a less-than-ideal audience, someone on the team is going to argue you tested with the wrong audience, and you'll have to run the test again. Remember, we want to design our tests to learn as much as we can from failures.

CHAPTER ELEVEN

MEASURING IMPACT

"Your delusions, no matter how convincing, will
wither under the harsh light of data."
— Alistair Croll and Benjamin Yoskovitz, *Lean Analytics*

I was excited to join AfterCollege as their Vice President of Product and Design. AfterCollege helps new college graduates find their first job out of school. I had experience in the recruiting industry, but little experience with this particular customer segment, so I kicked off my continuous-interviewing habit during the first week on the job.

Right away, I learned something surprising. I asked college seniors to tell me about their experience looking for a job. Most expressed the same sentiment over and over again. The vast majority of job boards (including ours) asked students two questions: 1) What type of job do you want? 2) In what location? Unfortunately, most of the students that I talked to didn't know how to answer either of these questions. They had no idea what types of jobs they were qualified for, and they were open to living in many places. The average 22-year-old doesn't have enough work experience to even be aware of what types of jobs exist, and they have the location flexibility to go where the best opportunities are. Some had a preference to return home or to stay near their college town, but about half were willing to go anywhere. It didn't take long for me to realize this was a huge problem. We had to stop asking college students questions they couldn't answer.

As a product team, we realized that we had proprietary data that could help us solve this problem. We had years of behavioral data about which types of jobs students applied to, and, more importantly, we knew from working with employers what types of students they wanted for different types of jobs. In other words, we were in a great position to tell students what types of jobs they were qualified for if they told us what they studied.

Instead of asking, "What type of job do you want?" and "Where do you want to work?" we realized we could ask students, "Where do you go to school?" "What are you studying?" and "When do you plan to graduate?" We suspected these questions would be much easier for students to answer, and we thought we could use their answers to recommend jobs to them.

Our long-term vision was to develop a machine-learning algorithm that matched students to the best jobs based on their own preferences and what we knew employers wanted. But before we invested in a machine-learning algorithm (we didn't know anything about machine learning yet), we needed to learn if this idea was worth investing in. It was so different from what everyone else was doing, we needed to make sure it would work.

To build a quick prototype, we realized that, as working professionals, we had more experience with job types than most college seniors and that we could create a crude approximation of our matching algorithm by creating saved searches for each of the areas of study in our system. Instead of having a sophisticated machine-learning algorithm behind the scenes, we simply crafted search queries ourselves. For example, if a student indicated they were an English major, we might search for marketing, content management, journalism, speech writing, and public-relations jobs.

It wouldn't be perfect, but we thought it would be better than what students were entering themselves.

We also knew it would help us quickly evaluate how successful our new idea might be. We had dozens of assumptions we wanted to test. Would college students trust our recommendations? Would they be open to exploring jobs they themselves didn't select? Would they be confused by our unique interface? After all, every other job board asked them to enter what type of job they wanted. Could we collect enough feedback to continue to refine our algorithm? Would our metrics show that this solution was better than what we currently had?

We knew we wanted to start small, as this idea was full of risk. So, we started by diverting a small percentage of our traffic to a new search page. Students entered their area of study, and we ran the relevant "saved search" behind the scenes. We were able to get this working prototype live in just a few days. We then watched what happened.

In our traditional "What type of job do you want?" interface, only 36% of students started a search. Two thirds of our site visitors never even started their job search. With our new "Tell us what you studied" interface, 83% of our visitors started their search. This was a huge improvement. Our new questions were much easier to answer, so more students were able to start their search.

But what happened after that? We found that students who entered job types and locations were more likely to view and apply for jobs, but not by much (only about 10%). We suspected it was because these students already had an inkling of what they wanted to do and where they wanted to work. But for everyone else, that interface simply didn't work. In our new interface, we saw a small drop-off in the number of searchers who viewed and applied for jobs, but we saw many more students start their search, so our overall performance was much better in the new interface. We knew right away it was safe to keep investing in this idea.

But where should we go from here? We didn't have a production-quality product. Remember, we tested with a crude prototype that we cobbled together in just a few days. We still had many more assumptions to test. We didn't feel like we were done with discovery. But we also were seeing better results with our prototype than we were with our production-quality product.

We debated about whether we should switch all of our traffic to the new prototype. We were seeing great results from our early assumptions tests, but we still had one key question to answer: Did our new idea drive our desired outcome? Our desired outcome wasn't to increase search starts, nor was it to increase job views or job applications. It was to increase the number of students getting jobs through our platform. We thought if we could get more students starting their search, we would increase the number of students who found jobs on our platform. But job views and applications aren't always leading indicators of hires. A student can view and apply to many jobs and never hear back from an employer. We needed to make sure that students were as likely (and hopefully, more likely) to find a job with our new interface as they were with our old interface. We decided we needed to continue to split our traffic until we could confirm that our new interface supported our desired outcome.

This story illustrates a few key lessons. First, it's easy to get caught up in successful assumption tests. The world is full of good ideas that will succeed on some level. However, an outcome-focused product trio needs to stay focused on the end goal—driving the desired outcome. We need to remember to measure not just what we need to evaluate our assumption tests, but also what we need to measure impact on our outcome.

Second, this story also highlights the iterative nature of discovery and delivery. Many teams ask, "When are we done with discovery? When do we get to send our ideas to delivery?" The answer to the first question is simple. You are never done with discovery. Remember, this book is about *continuous* discovery. There is always more to learn and to discover. The second question is harder to answer. In the AfterCollege story, we had already started the delivery work. Our prototype had a working interface that real customers could use. We were collecting real data. Our discovery required that we start delivery. Measuring the impact of that delivery resulted in us needing to do more discovery.

This is why we say discovery feeds delivery and delivery feeds discovery. They aren't two distinct phases. You can't have one without the other. In Chapter 10, you learned to iteratively invest in experiments, to start small, and to grow your investment over time. Inevitably, as your experiments grow, you are going to need to test with a real audience, in a real context, with real data. Testing in your production environment is a natural progression for your discovery work. It's also where your delivery work begins. If you instrument your delivery work, discovery will not only feed delivery, but delivery will feed discovery.

In this chapter, you'll learn how to instrument your product so that you can evaluate assumption tests using live prototypes. You'll learn how to measure the impact of your delivery work, using your desired outcome as your North Star. And you'll learn how to keep your discovery and delivery tightly coupled so that you never have to wonder if you are ready for delivery.

Don't Measure Everything

It's counterintuitive, but when instrumenting your product, don't try to measure everything from the start. You'll quickly get overwhelmed. You'll spend weeks debating what events to track, how to name your events, and who is responsible for what before you even get started. This is a waste of time. There is no way to know from the outset how you should set everything up. No matter how much planning you do, you'll make mistakes. You'll measure something that you thought meant one thing and discover later that it really meant something else. You'll develop a naming schema only to later discover that you forgot about a key part of the product. You'll find the perfect way to measure a key action only to learn months later that you had a bug that caused that event to trigger ten times more often than it should have. It happens to all of us. Trust that you'll learn as you go.

Instead of trying to plan everything upfront, start small, and experiment your way to the best instrumentation.

Instrument Your Evaluation Criteria

Start by instrumenting what you need to collect to evaluate your assumption tests. As you build your live prototypes[54], consider what you need to measure to support your evaluation criteria. Don't worry about measuring too much beyond that. For example, in the story that opens this chapter, we had several assumptions we needed to test:

- Students will start more searches if we ask them easier questions.
- Students will view jobs that we recommend.
- Students will apply to jobs that we recommend.

We defined evaluation criteria for each assumption:

- 250 out of 500 visitors will start their search using our new interface. (Remember, we were seeing only 180 out of 500, or 36%, start their search on our old interface. We wanted to see a big jump in search starts to warrant such a different interface.)

---

54 A live prototype is a prototype that you build and test in your production environment. It allows you to test with real customer data in an actual situation rather than in a simulated situation.

- At least 63 of our 500 students will view at least one job. (Our current interface was performing at 81 out of 500. We set our initial criteria lower, because we knew our canned searches weren't perfect, and we were confident we could improve them over time.)
- At least 7 of our 500 students would apply for a job. (Our current interface was performing at 12 out of 500. Again, we set our initial criteria lower because we knew our results would get better over time.)

With this evaluation criteria in mind, here's what we measured:

- # of people who visited the search start page
- # of people who started a search
- # of people who viewed at least one job
- # of people who applied for at least one job

Notice how we are counting the number of people who took a specific action and not counting the number of actions. This is an important distinction to pay attention to when instrumenting your product. Sometimes you'll want to count people. Other times you'll want to count actions. A good way to suss this out is to ask, "If one person did many actions, does that create as much value as many people doing one action?" If you need many people to take action, you'll want to count people. If it doesn't matter how many people take action, you'll want to count actions.

In this case, our assumptions were more about the perception of our new interface. We were concerned that students might not trust our recommendations. So, we wanted to measure how many people engaged with our job listings. We wanted to make sure that the new interface was working for more people than the old interface.

However, when we started to measure the relevance of our saved searches, we started to count actions. We wanted to know how

many jobs people found to be compelling. This wasn't a straightforward metric. If someone views 25 jobs, it might be because they
are finding 25 jobs that interest them. Or it might be because it
took 25 tries before a job interested them. For relevance, we took
two measurements. We measured the position of a job view in the
search result (e.g., a student viewed the first vs. third job in the
search results). We also measured the ratio of job views to job
applications (e.g., the number of jobs someone had to view before
they applied for a job).

Counting people helped us understand how many of our students
were having success on our platform. Counting actions helped us
understand how hard each student had to work to find success.

Notice, however, that we did not start by measuring everything.
We didn't track every click on every page. We started with our
assumptions, and we measured exactly what we needed to test
our assumptions.

Measure Impact on Your Desired Outcome

In addition to instrumenting what you need to evaluate your
assumption tests, you also want to measure what you need to evaluate your progress toward your desired outcome. Our outcome at
AfterCollege was to increase the number of students who found
jobs on our platform. For our assumption tests, we were measuring
search starts, job views, and job applications, but these metrics
were only leading indicators of our desired outcome.

Over time, we also wanted to move closer to measuring our
outcome itself, so that we could track progress week over week
and quarter over quarter. When I started at AfterCollege, we didn't
have a way of measuring how often a student got a job. We lost
track of students after they applied for a job. The post-apply steps
like interviewing, receiving an offer, and accepting an offer all happened off of our platform. We needed to find a way to incentivize

students to tell us when they got a job or employers to tell us when they made a hire.

Some people in the company argued that we should measure our success by job applications. After all, we had no control over who a company hired or how a student interviewed. But the number of job applications was an easy metric to game. It would be easy to encourage students to apply to many jobs, but this wouldn't necessarily increase their success of finding a job. If we wanted to measure the value we created for our customers, we knew we needed to measure when a student got a job. We couldn't be afraid to measure hard things.

Since most college students have little to no interviewing experience, nor do they know how to negotiate offers, we decided that we could use this lack of knowledge to help us measure what happens after they completed an application. Twenty-one days after a student applied for a job, we sent the student an email and asked them what happened. The email gave them four options:

1. "I never heard back." If they selected this option, we encouraged them to find new jobs to apply to.
2. "I got an interview." If they selected this option, we gave them tips for how to prepare for their interview.
3. "I got an offer." If they selected this option, we gave them tips on how to evaluate and negotiate their offer.
4. "I got the job." If they selected this option, we congratulated them.

Not everyone replied to our email. In fact, when we first launched it, only 5% of job applications (not applicants) netted a reply to the email. But over time, we grew that to 14%, and, by the time I left, we were at a 37% response rate. That's not perfect, but it gave us some visibility into what was happening after an application. I know that if we had kept iterating on that email, the response rate would have continued to improve. We probably would have experimented with other ways of collecting the same data. We knew that, if we were relentless, we would find a way to track our desired outcome.

Here's the key lesson. Just because the hire wasn't happening on our platform didn't mean it wasn't valuable for us to measure it. We knew it was what would create value for our students, our employees, and ultimately our own business. So, we chipped away at it. We weren't afraid to measure hard things—and you shouldn't be, either.

Revisiting Different Types of Outcomes

In Chapter 3, we distinguished between business outcomes, product outcomes, and traction metrics as a way to help us set the scope for our product work. In the AfterCollege story, our product outcome was to improve search starts, and we succeeded at doing that. But our business outcome was to increase the number of students who found jobs on our platform. We had to continue to instrument our product to evaluate if driving our product outcome had the intended impact on our business outcome. This work took longer than expected. We didn't want to wait to have the final answer before pushing value to our customers, so we continued to experiment in our production environment. Our discovery continued through to delivery.

This isn't uncommon. However, in the AfterCollege story, it was easy for us to experiment in production. We were able to get a working prototype live in only a few days. Let's return to our streaming-entertainment example to work through a more complex case. We can learn a lot about our subscribers' interest in sports by running the assumption tests we defined in Chapter 10. However, to test if adding sports will drive our product outcome (to increase average minutes watched) and our business outcome (to increase subscriber retention), we'll need to find small ways to experiment with real data—in other words, in our production environment.

We can't test if watching sports on our platform will increase viewer minutes until we have sports on our platform. This might look like a Catch-22, but it's not. We don't need to test with the full solution to evaluate the impact on our outcomes. For example, we could partner with a local channel to stream one sporting event on one day and evaluate the impact on viewing minutes for the subscribers who watched that sporting event. We can look at whether their overall viewing minutes went up, or if they cut out content in other areas to make time for the sporting event. Integrating all local-channel content might require new business partnerships, contracts to be signed, and APIs to be developed. But starting with one event might allow you to circumvent a good chunk of that work, allowing both parties to test their assumptions before they commit to a longer-term agreement.

Just like in the AfterCollege story, it might take even more time to evaluate if sports content will drive the business outcome (increased subscriber retention). Streaming one sporting event likely won't have a noticeable impact on subscriber numbers. However, if it impacts viewer minutes, we can keep investing, working on the belief that increasing viewing minutes will increase subscriber retention. The key in both examples is to remember to track the long-term connection between your product outcome and your business outcome. If, over time, an increase in viewing minutes doesn't lead to an increase in subscriber retention, then the team will need to find a new product outcome that *does* drive the business outcome.

Avoid These Common Anti-Patterns

As you work to instrument your product and understand the impact of your product changes on your desired outcomes, avoid these common anti-patterns.

Getting stuck trying to measure everything. By far the most common mistake teams make when instrumenting their product is that they turn it into a massive waterfall project, in which they think they can define all of their needs upfront. Instead, start small. Instrument what you need to evaluate this week's assumption tests. From there, work toward measuring the impact of your product changes on your product outcome. And with time, work to strengthen the connection between your product outcome and your business outcome.

Hyperfocusing on your assumption tests and forgetting to walk the lines of your opportunity solution tree. It's exhilarating when our solutions start to work. It feels good when customers engage with what we build. But sadly, satisfying a customer need is not our only job. We need to remember that our goal is to satisfy customer needs while creating value for our business. We are constrained by driving our desired outcome. This is what allows us to create viable products, and viable products allow us to continue to serve our customers. So, when you find a compelling solution, remember to walk the lines of your opportunity solution tree. Desirability isn't enough. Viability is the key to long-term success.

Forgetting to test the connection between your product outcome and your business outcome. Unfortunately, it's not enough to drive product outcomes. The connection between our product outcome and our business outcome is a theory that needs to be tested. As you build a history of driving a product outcome, you need to remember to evaluate if driving the product outcome is, in turn, driving the business outcome. It's what keeps our businesses thriving, allowing us to continue to serve our customers.

CHAPTER TWELVE

MANAGING THE CYCLES

"Trusting the process can give you the confidence to take risks."
— Chip and Dan Heath, *Decisive*

Thus far, we've worked our way through the continuous discovery habits sequentially. We started by defining a clear desired outcome, we interviewed to discover opportunities, we visually captured and synthesized what we were learning with experience maps and opportunity solution trees, we prioritized a target opportunity, we brainstormed solutions, we identified our hidden assumptions, we rapidly tested those assumptions, and we continued to measure impact all the way through delivery. It's easy to think that, if we simply follow the process, we'll come out the other side with a product that customers love. Unfortunately, it's not that simple. The reality is this process is a messy, winding path with lots of twists and turns. Most of the work in discovery is not following the process—it's managing the cycles.

In this chapter, I'll highlight stories of real product teams who, throughout the course of their discovery work, learned something surprising along the way. The surprise required that they stop charging forward and instead loop back to a previous step. You'll meet a team at Simply Business, a UK-based insurance company, who learned after testing a series of solutions that their opportunity wasn't as important to their customers as they had originally reported. You'll meet a team at CarMax who tackled an evergreen opportunity by breaking it up into sub-opportunities and used assumption testing to figure out what they could do now versus what they might have to push off to later. You'll meet a team at Farm Credit Services of America who uncovered a key value proposition that could have put their entire outcome at risk, but instead used their discovery work to drive the outcome while preserving the value proposition. And finally, you'll meet a team at Snagajob who had the luxury of embedding with a customer and how they used that opportunity to improve customer satisfaction across their customer base.

As you read through these stories, pay particular attention to how and when the teams had to loop back to an earlier habit to help them get unstuck or to work around a new constraint. Notice how, despite these surprises, it was the same core discovery habits that helped them find their way.

Simply Business: Not All Opportunities Need Solutions

Mina Kasherova, a Senior Product Manager at Simply Business, and her team kept hearing about the same pain point in most of their customer interviews: the havoc of late client payments. Simply Business is one of the UK's biggest business-insurance providers, specializing in public-liability insurance for small-to-midsize enterprises and insuring more than 750,000 small businesses, landlords, and not-for-profit organizations. Many of Simply Business's customers are freelancers and small-business owners who often struggle with clients not paying invoices on time, creating financial strain. Not only did the team hear about this pain point in a number of their customer interviews, but they also had market research and government data that suggested that late payments were a top problem for small businesses.

When Mina's team started assessing and prioritizing the opportunity space, choosing this opportunity as their target opportunity was a no-brainer. They generated several solutions and identified a diverse set of three to test: 1) articles to educate small-businesses owners on how to prevent late payments, 2) the ability to offer discounts for early payments, and 3) a service that automated payment collection.

Within a week, they were able to launch three assumption tests, one for each idea. To test if their customers were willing to read content about how to prevent late payments, they integrated a couple of existing blog articles about late payments onto their customer-account page and measured how many customers clicked through to read them. For invoice discounting and automatic payment collection, their riskiest assumptions were around the complexity of each of these ideas. They wanted to start by testing if customers understood each of the offerings. They mocked up a summary of each program and used an unmoderated usability-testing tool to ask small-business owners who had recently had challenges with late payments to read through the summary and explain what they thought each program offered. They then asked each participant to explain if the offering would have helped them collect on their most recent late payment. They were primarily interested in evaluating if the participants fully understood the benefits of each solution.

Unfortunately, the first assumption test failed. A very small percentage of customers clicked through to read the articles about how to prevent late payments. The team was concerned that the customer-account page might not be the right place to integrate the content and started to brainstorm other places to share the content. But they stopped once they watched the videos from their other two tests. Not only did most participants struggle to understand the solutions, but most also expressed that, while they had issues with late payments, they weren't interested in third-party help in solving the problem. They each expressed that they had strong relationships with their clients, and they felt that removing themselves from the collections process would harm the relationship.

This was a big surprise for Mina's team. Even though they had heard late payments come up as a pain point in interview after interview and they had market research reinforcing what they had heard, the results of their assumption tests were clear. Their customers did not want Simply Business to help them with this problem. Now, to be clear, this doesn't mean there wasn't a real need here. However, the team realized it wasn't a need that they could address in the short term. It was no longer the highest-impact opportunity that they should tackle next.

Thankfully, Mina's team had a strong habit of weekly interviews. So, when they revisited their opportunity solution tree to choose a new target opportunity, they weren't starting from scratch. Their tree continued to evolve as they ran their assumption tests, and they already had a clear idea of what opportunity might be next. You might remember Raya Raycheva's comment about the value of continuous interviewing from Chapter 5: "We killed an opportunity on Tuesday, chose a new one on Wednesday, and used our already-scheduled interviews on Thursday to learn about the new opportunity." Raya was the User Research Lead on Mina's team.

Mina and her team's story illustrates why it's so important not to get bogged down in analysis paralysis when assessing and prioritizing opportunities. All the data pointed in one direction, but when they started assumption testing, they collected another piece of the puzzle that completely changed the landscape. That's going to happen. Fortunately, because Mina's team moved quickly, they invested only a week into an opportunity that wasn't going to be fruitful. Compare that to the weeks or months that many teams spend building the wrong features, and this hiccup is no big deal. Mina's team also had the discipline and the wisdom to recognize when they were going down a troublesome path, and they quickly course-corrected. These course-corrections should be celebrated. The fruit of discovery work is often the time we save when we decide *not* to build something.

CarMax: The Importance of Now, Next, Future

As Senior Product Manager on the CarMax Digital Merchandising Experience team, Victoria Lawson was focused on displaying cars in a way that would ignite desire and ultimately lead customers to purchase a car. She compares the user experience to a dating site, where the goal is for a customer to "find the right one and make a commitment," only in CarMax's case, it's with a vehicle rather than another human being.

Through the course of customer interviews, Victoria's team identified the target opportunity: "I want to feel confident that this car is in good condition." Additionally, they saw new competitors start to highlight the cosmetic condition of their vehicles by visually indicating where a vehicle had dings, dents, or scratches, and Victoria's team was hearing from consumers that they appreciated having this information. Many product teams would simply copy what their competitors were doing, but for Victoria's team, it wasn't that simple. A key value proposition for CarMax vehicles is that they go through an inspection-and-reconditioning process that fixes many of the cosmetic issues that their competitors were highlighting. Odds are, if a competitor is highlighting a ding on a vehicle, CarMax couldn't highlight that same ding on their vehicle, because they would have fixed it in their reconditioning process. Would consumers understand that CarMax wasn't highlighting dings, dents, and scratches because they had fixed them?

Victoria's team had several questions they needed to answer before they could tackle this opportunity. While consumers were saying they valued the cosmetic condition of a vehicle, Victoria's team didn't want to take this for granted. They started by testing how much cosmetic conditioning impacted a consumer's purchase decision. To test whether customers were accurately describing their own priorities, Victoria's team set up a test in which they had wireframe versions of the same car—one had minor cosmetic issues and was $1,000 cheaper, while the other had no cosmetic issues but cost $1,000 more. Through this testing, they learned that people were willing to pay more for cars that were cosmetically reconditioned. This was a key learning, because it meant that CarMax's reconditioning value proposition was important to customers.

Next, they had to figure out how to communicate this value proposition to their customers. Victoria's team had two primary strategies for how they might do this. They could try to address the opportunity by highlighting the value of CarMax's inspection-and-reconditioning program (a more generalized approach), or they could address it by sharing vehicle-specific reconditioning information (e.g., "A ding was removed"). Due to the volume of cars CarMax sells and the work that would be required to test vehicle-specific concepts, Victoria's team knew that the quickest path to drive customer value would be to leverage general reconditioning to solve this opportunity, and wanted to prioritize discovery in that space before exploring larger efforts around vehicle-specific solutions.

Victoria's team knew that customers primarily evaluated cosmetic condition by viewing photos of the car. So, they experimented with adding text overlays on top of the images that highlighted CarMax's reconditioning work (e.g., "No major dings or dents"). The image gallery is one of the most engaged areas on the page, so the team established a high test threshold to ensure that they were truly solving the customer opportunity and could justify the high-visibility placement of the content. However, after several experiments, they were still unable to meet the test thresholds. Their changes did help consumers build trust in CarMax's inspection-and-reconditioning process, but they were still hearing from consumers that they wanted vehicle-specific information to truly build confidence in a specific car's condition. After a series of attempts, Victoria's team concluded that they had done as much as they could at this moment in time to address their target opportunity. They learned that, to really solve it, they would need to consider vehicle-specific solutions. Since these types of solutions would require a much larger investment from multiple teams, Victoria's team knew that, to deliver solutions to truly meet their customer needs, they would need to push this opportunity into the future.

Victoria's team story is a great example of the temporal nature of opportunity selection. While we might assume that we'll tackle all of the opportunities on our trees with time, there are some opportunities that are a better fit to tackle right now vs. in the future. Victoria's team chose an opportunity that they thought they could tackle quickly by leveraging CarMax's strong brand, however, they learned that consumers really needed vehicle-specific solutions and, as a result, the team had to defer this particular opportunity to later. Again, it turned out fine. Victoria's team simply went back to assessing and prioritizing the opportunity space and chose a new short-term target opportunity. They were still able to make short-term progress toward their desired outcome, while laying the groundwork for even more impact down the road. With time, their discovery work helped them successfully make the case to invest in vehicle-specific solutions. Today, they are able to integrate vehicle-specific data about parts that were replaced during their reconditioning process, which reinforces CarMax's reconditioning value proposition with its customers. Many teams shy away from hard problems—it's easier to focus on low-hanging fruit. But Victoria's story shows the value of balancing the short-term with the long-term. They looked for quick wins, but when they didn't pan out, they used their discovery work to make the case to go after the harder solutions.

FCSAmerica: Balancing Customer Value With Business Needs

Carl Horne is the VP of Digital Products & Services at Farm Credit Services of America (FCSAmerica). When farmers, ranchers, or other agri-businesses need credit or other financial services, they go to FCSAmerica. And this is a big decision, because agriculture requires a lot of capital (most loans range from several hundred thousand to several million dollars).

Carl's team had the goal of engaging with customers digitally. This was a broad goal that could be interpreted in many different ways, but they chose to focus on the website experience. FCSAmerica had traditionally provided a high-touch personal experience, so business leaders wondered if they could make some of their resources self-service. But this led to a potential problem. Customers regularly shared that they liked talking to their financial officer, and they considered this to be a trusted relationship. Would customers be willing to give up that trusted relationship for the convenience of a digital experience?

Through the course of customer interviews, Carl's team learned that many of their customers were already researching online to figure out how much property they could afford. This led Carl's team to identify "What can I afford?" as an opportunity that they might be able to address digitally.

They experimented to figure out how to address this opportunity with an online calculator. The idea was that a potential customer could enter the relevant information and the calculator would provide the answer, similar to an online mortgage calculator. In this scenario, the calculator would be a self-serve option for customers.

But since they'd heard from customers that human interaction was important, Carl's team was concerned that an online calculator might not be sufficient. Would customers trust the results? Or would they still seek advice from their financial officer? They experimented with offering a chat feature alongside the calculator so a person would be online during business hours to answer customers' questions live. These experiments demonstrated clearly that customers did not want to talk to a person at this stage of the application process. No matter what they did to change the wording or the images, customers would consistently close out of the browser to avoid interacting via chat.

Through these experiments, Carl's team came to two critical conclusions: The human touch wasn't needed during the calculation stage—it was more important later in the process—and the opportunity of "What can I afford?" was something Carl's team could solve digitally.

They iteratively built the online calculator, and, today, that product has grown into their successful FarmLend program, a service that enables farmers and ranchers to apply online—rather than through their branches—for financing. Carl's team was able to identify an existing need where their customers were already comfortable engaging online and used that as a starting point to teach their customers how to engage digitally. Their FarmLend customers still engage with and benefit from a trusted relationship with their financial officer, but they do much more of the loan process digitally through the FarmLend website.

Snagajob: Iterating Through Small Opportunities for Big Impact

At Snagajob, an hourly work marketplace, Product Manager Amy O'Callaghan and Product Designer Jenn Atkins were always trying to solve one core problem: How could they connect people who need work with the people who need workers in a satisfying way for both parties?

In an attempt to answer that question, Amy and Jenn were working on improving their net promoter score (NPS) as their desired outcome. They dove into NPS comments and interview feedback and identified several opportunities. Two of these opportunities were already very familiar: "I don't have enough applications" and "I don't have the right applications." But they were surprised to uncover a brand-new opportunity: "I can't get in touch with my candidates." As they spoke with hiring managers, Amy and Jenn discovered that they could rarely connect with candidates on the phone. Only about one in ten candidates answered the phone when a hiring manager called, and hardly any of them returned the call after receiving a voicemail message from a hiring manager.

Through their customer interviews, Amy and Jenn learned that this was an issue with *every* applicant from *all* hiring platforms—not just Snagajob. This meant they had a "big, hairy problem that no one understood, which would be a major, multi-faceted win for us if we solved it."

But the challenge with a "big, hairy problem," as Amy and Jenn describe it, is that it can be difficult to address. Where do you even start?

The way Amy and Jenn approached it was by going on "walka-bouts" to nearby retail stores and restaurants and asking to speak to the hiring manager. Through these conversations, they started establishing relationships with local business owners, asking about their hiring needs and offering to be their unpaid, personal hiring assistants, typically for a 30-day period. Describing this experience, they say, "It was exhausting, illuminating, and amazing."

Through their in-depth research, Amy and Jenn discovered a number of smaller sub-opportunities that helped them better understand why hiring managers were struggling to get in touch with candidates. One of their first big discoveries was that calling candidates was ineffective. Amy and Jenn ran a quick test that proved that, even when a candidate said they preferred phone calls, they were unlikely to answer a call from a hiring manager. Through experimentation, they realized that the applicant's persona had fundamentally changed. They were mobile first. They preferred texting to talking on the phone. Many of them didn't even have their voicemail set up properly.

When Amy and Jenn pivoted to texting candidates, they saw an immediate improvement in response rate. First, they would text to ask if it was a good time to call *before* calling a candidate. When that went well, they began exploring other ways to communicate via text—most often attempting to ask follow-up questions and schedule interviews. They tried sending texts both as people and as bots, but quickly realized this was only a temporary solution, since most hiring managers would not want to use their personal devices to text candidates.

They knew that, to solve this problem, it had to work for both the candidates and the hiring manager. So, they started looking for mobile-first, web-accessible tools that allowed managers to communicate via text and candidates to answer from a phone. They would send a text asking candidates if they'd be willing to answer a few follow-up questions on their application. If they answered "Yes," they would send them a link to a SurveyMonkey form. This was easy to set up and fill out on a mobile device. This small tweak allowed them to connect with candidates in a way that simply wasn't happening before.

Once they were able to successfully connect hiring managers with candidates, they discovered the next problem: Finding a time to schedule interviews required a lot of back and forth. Amy and Jenn continued making small iterations and improvements like these until, finally, they had a well-oiled interview-scheduling machine. And once they tackled that, they learned about the next hurdle: Interview no-shows. But they continued to chip away at one opportunity at a time. Looking back, they can't say that one single opportunity was responsible for their success, but marching across their tree one opportunity at a time is what allowed them to deliver on their desired outcome.

Amy's and Jenn's story illustrates how iteratively tackling small opportunities can add up to have a large impact on an outcome. When first getting started, it can be hard to see how starting with a small problem will ever amount to anything. But if you keep at it and work the cycles, small changes start to snowball, and you start to see the collective impact of working across your tree. Addressing sub-opportunities over time eventually addresses parent opportunities. And addressing parent opportunities is your path to consistently driving product outcomes.

Avoid These Common Anti-Patterns

As you manage the cycles of continuous discovery, be sure to avoid these common anti-patterns.

Overcommitting to an opportunity. Throughout your discovery, you will uncover opportunities that are important to your customers that you won't be able to deliver on. We saw this in Mina's story at Simply Business. It's quite possible that someone else will solve late payments for small-business owners. It may even be a Simply Business competitor who does so. However, given the context in which Mina's team was working—what her company was asking of her and what she was learning from her customers—it turned out not to be the right opportunity for her right now. This doesn't mean her team can't return to it later down the road.

We also saw this come up in Victoria's story. Her team had the resources to address the need in a specific way—with CarMax generalized data, not vehicle-specific data. When they learned that generalized data wasn't sufficient, they chose a new target opportunity instead of continuing with an opportunity that they knew they weren't in a position to address right now.

One of the hardest challenges with opportunity selection is identifying the right opportunity for right now. However, a round of assumption tests should help you assess fit quickly. These stories are a good reminder of why we want to run quick tests rather than overinvest in the best tests.

Avoiding hard opportunities. Some teams interpret continuous delivery to mean continuous delivery of easy solutions. Quick wins have a time and a place in our work If we can deliver impact this week, we should. However, many of the opportunities we uncover will take time to address adequately. Don't confuse quick testing and iterative delivery with easy solutions. You saw in Chapter 11 that, at AfterCollege, we were able to find a quick test of a hard solution. Before we invested months into building a robust machine-learning solution, we started with a crude approximation that we could prototype in a few days.

We also saw this mindset in Victoria's story. When her team learned that they had tapped as much of the potential as they could out of generalized data, they didn't shirk away from vehicle-specific data. They started to lay the groundwork for those types of solutions by working with other teams. In the meantime, they worked another opportunity in parallel. This allowed them to both deliver impact now *and* lay the groundwork for even more impact in the future.

Drawing conclusions from shallow learnings. As you learned in Chapter 2, discovery requires strong critical-thinking skills. Otherwise, it's easy to draw fast conclusions from shallow learnings. We saw this in Carl's FarmLend story. Once hearing that customers valued picking up the phone to talk to their loan officer, Carl's team could have abandoned their digital-engagement strategy. But instead, they asked the harder question, "How can we reconcile our business need with our customers' needs?" And as a result, they found an opportunity where their customers *did* want to engage digitally, and they used that opportunity to grow their digital relationship with their customers. They did the work to uncover the depth behind their shallow learning. Their customers did value their relationship with their financial officer. But they were also willing to do plenty of research on their own. Carl's team worked to tease out these nuances and were rewarded for it.

Giving up before small changes have time to add up. While you do want to measure the impact of your product changes, don't expect to see large step-function results from every change. Oftentimes it takes a series of changes to move the needle on our outcome. We saw this in Amy's and Jenn's story at Snagajob. Every time they solved one problem, it opened the door to the next problem. But they kept at it and, over time, had a big impact on their desired outcome.

CHAPTER THIRTEEN

SHOW YOUR WORK

*"The more leaders can understand where teams are, the
more they will step back and let teams execute."*
— Melissa Perri, *Escaping the Build Trap*

Lisa Orr, a product manager at Airship, and her team were tasked
with solving a recurring problem for their sales team. In conversation after conversation, prospects kept asking for a custom-
er-journey-builder feature that Airship didn't have. The simple
solution would have been to build what their competitors offered.
But Lisa and her team knew better. They were right in the middle of my 12-week coaching program and had learned that what
customers ask for isn't always what they need. They didn't want
to spend time, money, and energy building the wrong feature, so
instead, they turned to their discovery habits to help them out.

Airship started as a mobile push-notification company and
quickly expanded to a broader set of marketing-automation tools.
They help their customers send the right message to the right user
at the right time on the right channel. Odds are, if you've received
a push notification from AccuWeather about severe weather alerts,
a mobile boarding pass from Alaska Airlines, or a text message
from Boston Market about Rotisserie Rewards, it was delivered
by Airship. Airship operates in a crowded marketplace, and, as

marketing automation has matured and evolved, Airship, like most players in this space, has had to hustle to keep up.

When Lisa's team was asked to build a customer-journey builder to help Airship win deals against competitors who offered this feature, they knew they had a lot to learn. They started by interviewing their own customers who also used a competitor's journey builder. A journey builder allows a marketer to sequence marketing messages over time and across channels. For example, a retailer might design a post-purchase journey that starts with sending a purchase receipt by email. A few days later, the customer might receive a coupon via a push notification incentivizing them to return to the store. And upon entering the store, the customer might receive a text message reminding them to use their coupon.

In conversations with customers, Lisa's team quickly realized existing customer-journey builders weren't very good. They were so complex that many marketers didn't know how to get started. The customers who *did* ended up creating complicated journeys that were redundant and hard to maintain. It quickly became clear that building what the competitors offered wasn't going to be good enough. Lisa's team also realized that this was a huge opportunity to differentiate their offering from the competitors'.

Lisa's team interviewed customers, mapped out the opportunity space, explored multiple solutions, quickly prototyped to test their assumptions, and landed on a solution that they were excited about. However, when they shared their progress with the rest of the company, they ran into a significant roadblock. The sales team pushed back. They didn't want to sell something new. They wanted to give their prospects what they were asking for—a journey builder just like what the competition offered.

Thankfully, this story has a happy ending. Lisa and her team were able to convince their leadership to allow them to run a one-month beta launch with a limited set of customers to test out their new feature. They were confident, from having done good discovery, that, if they could just get customers using the feature, the sales team would be convinced. It turns out they were, and, after a successful beta release, the Airship Journeys product launched and has seen great success.

What I want to highlight here is that, while Lisa's team did a great job executing on their discovery and were able to bring a successful product to market, all that work would have gone to waste if they weren't able to get their sales team (and other business stakeholders) on board. This is a common tale and one that most product trios can learn from. It's not enough to do good discovery if you aren't bringing your stakeholders along with you. This chapter will show you how to use the same visual artifacts you learned throughout this book to help you manage and bring stakeholders along, so that, when you land on a better solution, the organization is ready and eager to adopt it.

Don't Jump Straight to Your Conclusions

When preparing for a meeting with stakeholders, we tend to focus on our conclusions—our roadmap, our release plan, our prioritized backlog. More often than not, this is exactly what our stakeholders are asking us to share. Even in companies that espouse a focus on outcomes, we still tend to spend most of our time talking about outputs.

The challenge with this approach is that our stakeholders often have their own conclusions. It's easy to have an opinion about outputs. We all have our own preferences about how a product or service should work. When we anchor the conversation in the solution space, we encourage our stakeholders to share their own preferences. However, these preferences aren't always grounded in good discovery. After all, it's our job to do discovery, not our stakeholders'.

When you frame the conversation in the solution space, you are framing the conversation to be about your opinion about what to build versus your stakeholders' opinion about what to build. If your stakeholders are more senior to you, odds are their opinion is going to win. This is why we have the dreaded HiPPO acronym (the Highest Paid Person's Opinions) and the saying "The HiPPO always wins." Many product trios complain about the HiPPO but miss the role they play in creating this situation.

When we present our conclusions, we aren't sharing the journey we took to reach those conclusions. Instead, we are inviting our stakeholders to an opinion battle—a battle we have no chance of winning.

Slow Down and Show Your Work

When meeting with stakeholders, don't start with your conclusions. Instead, slow down and show your work. Throughout this book, you've learned to use an opportunity solution tree to help you chart the best path to your desired outcome. This same visual can help you share your work with your stakeholders. Just like it's easy for us to get distracted by shiny new ideas, it's also easy for our stakeholders to get distracted. It's our job to set the context for how product decisions are made. Your opportunity solution tree helps you do exactly that. And just like it helped you and your team build confidence in your decisions, it will do the same for your stakeholders.

When meeting with stakeholders, start at the top of your tree. Remind your stakeholders what your desired outcome is. Ask them if anything has changed since you last agreed to this outcome. This sets the scope for the conversation.

Share how you mapped out the opportunity space. Highlight the top-level opportunities. Drill into the detail only when and where they ask for it. Ask them if you missed anything. Consider that they may have knowledge of opportunities that you might have missed. Capture their suggestions. You can always vet them in your future customer interviews.

Share how you assessed and prioritized the opportunity space. Use the tree structure to walk through each decision you made. Choose the appropriate level of detail based on the stakeholder you are talking to. Ask them if they would have made a different decision at each decision point. Consider their feedback.

Share more context about your target opportunity. Help them fully understand the customer need or pain point you intend to address. Use your interview snapshots to help your stakeholders empathize with your customers. Answer their questions. This step is critical. Your stakeholder needs to fully understand the opportunity you are pursuing before you share solutions with them. This is what sets the context for how to evaluate solutions and moves the conversation away from opinions and preferences.

Share the solutions you generated. Ask them if they have any of their own ideas. Make sure you capture and consider them. Share the set of three solutions you plan to move forward with. Ask them if they would have chosen a different set. Stay open-minded. You may have invested time and energy into your solution set, but remember: Solution ideas are a dime a dozen. The key criteria for your first solution set is diversity. Your stakeholders can often help you generate more diverse ideas than what your team can do on their own. If that's the case, don't be afraid to swap in some of their ideas.

If you've already started assumption testing, share your story maps and your assumption lists. Make sure your stakeholders fully understand how each solution might work. Remember, this is where opinions and preferences might pop up again. Gently remind your stakeholders what your target opportunity is. Ask your stakeholders to add to your assumption lists. This is where their unique knowledge and expertise can be invaluable for helping us catch our own blind spots.

Share your assumption map. Be sure to add any of the assumptions that your stakeholders identified. Ask them if they would have prioritized the assumptions differently. Make adjustments as needed.

Share your assumption tests. If you have data, share the data. Otherwise, share your execution plans. Ask for feedback. Consider and integrate their feedback.

Repeat.

When we show our work, we are inviting our stakeholders to co-create with us. Instead of sharing our conclusions and inviting them to share their preferences, we are sharing our work and inviting them to assess our thinking and to add their own. We are leveraging their expertise and improving our process.

Finally, I described this process as a one-time event. But a good product trio knows to continuously manage stakeholders. Share your work along the way, rather than all at the end. Be thoughtful about when and how to share your work. Some stakeholders will want all the details week over week; others might want the highlights monthly. Adapt to what your stakeholders need. But even if they ask for outputs, take the time to show the work that helped you conclude those were the right outputs.

Generate and Evaluate Options

When we take the time to show our work, using visual artifacts like experience maps, opportunity solution trees, and story maps, we are inviting our stakeholders along for the journey with us. Instead of presenting our conclusion—this is the roadmap, release plan, and backlog that will help us reach our desired outcome—we are presenting the potential paths we might take to get there. We are inviting our stakeholders to help us choose the right path. Instead of presenting a conclusion, we are generating and evaluating options. This allows our stakeholders to be a part of the process.

We are inviting them to co-create with us, which leads to much more buy-in and long-term success.

Common Anti-Patterns

As you work with your stakeholders, keep these common anti-patterns in mind.

Telling instead of showing. Even though we all know that showing is better than telling, all too often, we fall into the trap of telling instead of showing. We are proud of our work. We are excited about our conclusions. We love our ideas, so, of course, our stakeholders will love our ideas, too. We rush into telling our stakeholders everything we've learned instead of showing our stakeholders so that they can draw their own conclusions.

There's a cognitive bias that is coming into play when we do this. It's called the *curse of knowledge.*[55] Once we know something (like we do in this situation, we have a wealth of discovery work that supports our point of view), it's hard for us to remember what it was like not to have that knowledge. In fact, our conclusions—our roadmaps, our backlogs, our release plans—start to become obvious. We forget that not only are they not obvious to our stakeholders but also that they very likely have their own conclusions that seem obvious to them. The key to avoiding this "curse of knowledge" is to slow down. Start at the beginning. Walk your stakeholder through what you learned and what decisions you made. Give them space to follow your logic, and, most importantly, give them time to reach the same conclusion.

Overwhelming stakeholders with all the messy details. Even though we want to slow down and show our work, we don't want to overwhelm our stakeholders with every last detail of what we've

---

55   See this article by the Heath brothers (yup, the same Heath brothers who wrote *Decisive*) about the curse of knowledge: https://hbr.org/2006/12/the-curse-of-knowledge

learned. If you are interviewing customers and running several assumption tests every week, everything you are learning will quickly overwhelm a busy stakeholder.

Instead, you need to act as a smart filter. Tailor the detail and context to the stakeholder you are talking to. What does this stakeholder, in particular, need to know? Your boss might enjoy the discovery journey and want week-over-week updates of how things are going. Your marketing manager probably doesn't want that much detail. Instead, monthly updates with just the highlights might be adequate. Your CEO probably needs even less detail.

However, when someone wants less detail, it doesn't mean you aren't showing your work. Even with a busy CEO, you still want to start with the outcome you are driving, highlight the top two or three opportunities, give a quick explanation of why you chose the one you did, highlight your top solutions, and share the results of one or two assumption tests that support your final decision. For example, Lisa's team might share the following narrative: "Our goal is to reduce the number of lost sales from not having a journey builder (outcome). We interviewed customers and learned that existing journey builders are too complex; marketers don't know how to get started (opportunity one), and, when they do, their journeys are hard to maintain (opportunity two), and they often create redundant journeys (opportunity three). We decided to focus on reducing the complexity by helping marketers to zoom out from the messages they are sending to focus on the goals they are trying to achieve. We explored a few different ways to do this, but the most promising one is our lifecycle-maps idea. In testing, we found that marketers had no problem getting started and that they loved the high-level view on their work."

Of course, Lisa's team discovered dozens of opportunities, and their solutions addressed many of them. But their CEO doesn't need all of this detail. He needs to know that Lisa's team is finding a solution that customers love that drives the outcome he cares about.

Arguing with stakeholders about why their ideas won't work. As you do more and more assumption tests, assumptions become building blocks. You start to learn which building blocks will work and which won't. When you hear a new idea, you are going to be able to quickly assess it based on those building blocks. However, when working with stakeholders, we need to remember that they aren't starting from the same set of building blocks. The fastest way to discourage your stakeholders is to shoot down their ideas. Remember, nobody likes the know-it-all.

Instead of jumping straight to why an idea won't work, use your discovery framework to help the stakeholder see where their idea *does* fit. For example, is the stakeholder focused on a different outcome from you? If yes, then don't shoot down their idea. Even if you don't like the idea (remember, our preferences don't matter), you can remind your stakeholder that, while their idea might be a good fit for their outcome, it doesn't support your outcome right now. You can follow this same strategy if their solution addresses a different opportunity. You can always say something like, "That idea has promise. We'll consider it when we address that opportunity." You can even capture it on your tree or in your idea backlog (not your development backlog) so that you remember to return to it later.

If your stakeholder is suggesting a solution for your target opportunity, consider it. Should it be in your consideration set? If you can see that it is based on a faulty assumption, don't just call that out. Help your stakeholder reach that conclusion on their own. You can do this by story mapping their idea together. Generate assumptions together. When your stakeholder sees what assumptions their idea is based upon, you can now share what you've learned about those assumptions in your past assumption tests. This helps your stakeholder reach their own conclusions about their own ideas.

Trying to win the ideological battle instead of focusing on the decision at hand. No matter how strong your discovery process is, there will still be times when your stakeholders swoop in and ask you to do things their way. If they are more senior to you in the corporate hierarchy, that's their prerogative. What you can control is how you respond. I strongly recommend that you don't turn the conversation into an ideological battle. In fact, if you ever catch yourself saying, "This is the way it's supposed to be done," take a deep breath, and walk away from the conversation. You aren't going to win the ideological war in one conversation.

Instead, you need to take stock of the decision that needs to be made and focus on the best outcome given what you have to work with. Save the ideological war for later (or never). You aren't going to convince your stakeholder that their worldview is wrong. In fact, this is tied to the "Show, don't tell" advice above. When you are asked to deviate from your discovery process, telling your stakeholders that they are doing it wrong isn't going to get you anywhere. Focus on the opportunities with which you can show the benefit of working this way. Choose your battles. Don't fight the ones you can't win.

PART III

DEVELOPING YOUR CONTINUOUS DISCOVERY HABITS

CHAPTER FOURTEEN
START SMALL, AND ITERATE

"This all sounds great, but my company doesn't work this way."
— You, the reader

I was 22 years old. I had just graduated from college and was starting my first full-time job as an application software developer at HighWire Press, a division of the Stanford University Libraries and a pioneer in bringing STEM journals online. I was hired as a designer and front-end engineer working on several online communities for academic researchers. Our goal was to bring researchers from across disciplines (think biology, chemistry, medicine) who were working on the same types of problems together in a collaborative online space. We were working on innovative features like virtual folders to replace physical filing cabinets that stored decades of journal articles and message boards where researchers could discuss said journal articles. This was 1999, and the World Wide Web was the new frontier.

As a college student, I was introduced to human-centered design and was excited to put what I learned into practice on the job. I remember my first design assignment like it was yesterday. Our client, the American Association for the Advancement of Science (AAAS) was our collaborating partner on our first online community, and they had a long list of feature requests. My job was to design site navigation that encompassed all of those features. I spent a grand total of three days playing with different ideas and then walked into my first-ever client meeting.

I presented my designs, confident in my work (after all, my manager liked it), and waited for the accolades to roll in. That's when someone on the client side said, "This is horrible." It was a sucker punch. She continued, "This isn't what we want at all. Why can't you just do it like this?" At which point, she proceeded to describe what (unbeknown to me) she had asked for a few weeks prior before I joined the company. That's when I realized: I had no idea who our client was, what they wanted, or who their end-user was. What in the world was I doing throwing designs over the wall? So much for that high-priced, human-centered design education.

Actually, what that education gave me was the ability to bounce back. I knew that, while my boss (and the rest of the company) operated by throwing designs over the wall, it didn't mean I had to. I got to choose how I did my own work, and I knew if I was going to be good at design, I needed to keep the client and the end-user close. I started right then and there on that call. I invited the woman who was unhappy with my design to partner with me on the next iteration. We scheduled a phone call (this was before the days of Zoom) and agreed to work together.

From there, when I was asked to do design work, I joined the client meetings from the beginning of the project. I got involved at the contracting stage. I listened in when the client described what they wanted. I asked to attend their conferences. I spent time talking to the journal editors. I read the discussion forums in our product to learn more about end-users' research. I mined our feedback channels, looking for needs and pain points. I built feedback loops directly into the product. I didn't know how to get direct access to our end-users, so I looked for every proxy I could find.

This didn't happen overnight. I was 22. I had no idea what I was doing. I simply had a guiding principle: If I'm going to do good design work, I need to get close to my customer. That guiding principle stayed with me as I went on to work at early-stage startups; it's guided me as I started my own business, and it's helped me develop the coaching curriculum that this book is based on.

So why am I telling you this story? If you are reading this book and feel like these methods won't work at your company, here's what I'll tell you: I rarely had the support of senior leadership to do product discovery well. I worked at HighWire Press, where we let our clients dictate what we built for end-users. I worked at a startup where our Vice President of Product thought his job was to manage a spreadsheet of feature requests that came from the CEO. I worked at another startup where customers submitted requests and we built them. Trust me, I know what it's like to work at places that don't do modern product discovery.

However, in every single one of these jobs, I found a way to get close to the customer. I found a way to advocate for human-centered design. I found a way to build products that worked for our customers—and it wasn't that hard. Here's how I did it: I had a strong sense of agency.

I knew that I could impact how I did my own work. I didn't worry about what other people were doing. I didn't try to change the way these companies worked. I simply did my work my way, and I got results—so much so that, by the age of 32, I was the CEO of someone else's company. I don't share that to brag; I share that to show that you have more agency than you think you do.

Instead of asking for permission or waiting for someone to show you how, start small. Iterate from there. I made a career doing that, and I've coached hundreds of others to do the same. This chapter will help you get started on your own continuous-discovery journey, regardless of where your company is in its own transformation.

Build Your Trio

Don't work alone. The habits in this book are designed to be adopted by a cross-functional trio. Even if your team isn't fully resourced or your company culture doesn't support the trio model, you can start building these relationships yourself. If you are a product manager, find a designer and an engineer to partner with. Consult them on key decisions. Work together to decide what to build.

If your teammates change from project to project, your trio may change with it. That's okay.

If the first person you ask isn't interested, find someone who is. Start small with your ask. Instead of asking them to partner with you on all of your discovery decisions, ask them to weigh in on one small decision. Iterate from there.

If your company doesn't hire designers, find someone who is design-minded. Every company has people who naturally think from a usability perspective. Look for people who are good at simplifying complex concepts, have firsthand experience with your customers, and have an abundance of empathy for your customers' challenges.

Your guiding principle is simple: How can I include all three disciplines in as many discovery decisions as I can? Make next week look better than last week. Repeat.

Once you have your trio in place, you are ready to adopt the *keystone habit* of continuous discovery.

Start Talking to Customers

If you aren't familiar with the concept of a *keystone habit*, it comes from Charles Duhigg's book *The Power of Habit: Why We Do What We Do in Life and Business.* Duhigg argues, "Keystone habits start a process that, over time, transforms everything." They are habits that, once adopted, drive the adoption of other habits.

For most people, exercise is a keystone habit. When we exercise regularly, we naturally tend to eat better, we have more energy, and thus we are more productive at work. For others, making your bed each morning is a keystone habit. It sets the tone of rigor and discipline from the start of your day. This is why many military leaders advocate for this habit.

To be clear, it's not that exercise makes you eat better or making your bed makes you more disciplined, but doing the former makes the latter easier. The keystone habit builds motivation for the subsequent habits.

I've noticed this exact pattern emerge among product teams who develop a weekly habit of customer interviews. When product teams engage with their customers week over week, they don't just get the benefit of interviewing more often—they also start rapid prototyping and experimenting more often. They remember to doubt what they know and to test their assumptions. They do a better job of connecting what they are learning from their research activities with the product decisions they are making. This is why a weekly touchpoint with customers is a key part of the definition of continuous discovery that you were introduced to in Chapter 1.

I believe continuous interviewing is a keystone habit for continuous discovery. Of all the habits in this book, if you are looking for one place to get started, this is it.

If you're wondering how you're going to make this happen, I hear you. I've worked with dozens of teams who have genuinely struggled to find customers to talk to. They aren't allowed to build recruiting hooks into the product. Their sales and account-management teams want to own the relationship and be the go-between, rather than let product people have direct access. Their customers are busy doctors or secretive investors or high-powered CEOs. I can't tell you how to overcome all of these obstacles. I know from working with many teams that every situation is unique.

But I can tell you that there is a way. Even in the most challenging situations, the teams I've worked with have chipped away at getting more access to their customers. They've taken a continuous-improvement approach to the challenge. If they have never talked to a customer, they start small and try to find a single customer to talk to. If they can't do even that, they start by talking with someone who is similar to their customers. They use each conversation to get introduced to another person to talk to. They make next week look better than last week. And with time, they find themselves on a path to continuous interviewing.

No matter your situation, this is the habit to start with.

Work Backward

Many product teams aren't allowed to do discovery. They still work in a feature-team or delivery-team model, where business stakeholders tell them what to build. If this is you, don't worry—there is hope. Remember, I worked this way for years. You can still work on developing continuous discovery habits yourself.

When you are asked to deliver a specific solution, work backward. Take the time to consider, "If our customers had this solution, what would it do for them?" If you are talking to customers regularly, ask them. Try to uncover the implied opportunity. Even if it's a wild guess, starting to consider customer needs, pain points, and desires will help you deliver a better solution.

You can apply the same question to your business to uncover the implied outcome, "If we shipped this feature, what value would it create for our business?" Refine your answer until you get to a clear metric—that's your outcome. By the way, by asking those two questions, you've also built your first opportunity solution tree.

As you work on requirements for the solutions you were asked to build, remember to story map your ideas. Use your story maps to identify hidden assumptions. Even if you don't have the infrastructure to quickly prototype or test your assumptions, being aware of your assumptions will help you notice the evidence around you that either supports or refutes them. When you uncover a faulty assumption, work with your stakeholders to evolve the idea. Better yet, when a stakeholder brings a solution to you, story map and identify assumptions with them. The idea will improve right then and there.

Work with your stakeholders to identify the impact they expect a given feature to have. Document that conversation. As you implement the feature, be sure to instrument what you need to measure against the expected impact. Start doing post-release impact reviews with your stakeholders. Remind them what impact they *expected* a feature to have. Share with them the impact the feature *actually* had. If it falls short, as it inevitably will, share the implied opportunity you uncovered by asking, "Are we trying to solve this customer problem with this feature?" If your stakeholder agrees, ask if you can consider alternative solutions to that same customer need. Or better yet, ideate with your stakeholders. Congratulations! You just built out the first mini-branch of your opportunity solution tree.

The best time to advocate for discovery is when a feature falls short of expectations. You can gently suggest ways that you could have discovered the gap earlier in the process. This is a great time to share what you are learning in your interviews. But be careful. You don't want to come across as a know-it-all or have an "I told you so" attitude. Instead, approach the situation as a collaborative problem solver. Work with your stakeholders to evolve your processes. If they push back, let up. Remember, you don't have to worry about how other people work. You can make great strides yourself, focusing on how you work. But you'll be pleasantly surprised at how receptive folks are to small changes when things don't go as expected. Read the room, and adjust your suggestions accordingly.

Use Your Retrospectives to Reflect and Improve

Meet regularly as a trio to reflect on your discovery process. If you already do Scrum retrospectives, it's easy to add a couple of reflective questions to this meeting to also reflect on your discovery process.

I encourage my teams to ask, "What did we learn during this sprint that surprised us?" This could be anything from a feature release didn't have the expected impact, we learned a new insight in a customer interview, or we ran into a feasibility hurdle that required us to redesign a solution. Make a list.

Then, for each item on the list, ask, "How could we have learned that sooner?" The answers to these questions will help you improve your discovery process. If a release didn't have the intended impact, was there a faulty assumption that you neglected to uncover? Did it not get prioritized as one of your "leap of faith" assumptions for testing? If you learned a new insight during a customer interview, was it because you misunderstood a customer need, or did you uncover a new part of the customer experience for the first time? If you ran into a feasibility hurdle, is it because the requirements were misunderstood (maybe you need to revisit your story maps)? Or perhaps feasibility assumptions are a bit of a blind spot for your team.

As you conduct this retrospective, be nice to yourselves. Remember, no matter how good you get at discovery, you'll still run into surprises. Surprises help us improve. Take the time to learn from them.

Avoid These Common Anti-Patterns

As you work to adopt the continuous discovery habits, be sure to avoid these common anti-patterns.

Focusing on why a given strategy won't work (AKA "That will never work here"), instead of focusing on what is within your control. After every conference or meetup talk, participants always ask a question that falls into the form of, "That would never work at my company." It's easy to hear or read about what other companies do and think their tactics won't work at your company. It's true that every organization is unique. However, I've worked with teams in a variety of industries (from banking to healthcare to retail to marketing automation to security), at companies of all sizes (from two founders just getting started to global companies with hundreds of thousands of employees), on all types of products and services. The habits in this book have been adopted and worked at all of them. Do they need to be adapted to the unique organizational context? Absolutely! But in every instance, we were able to look at what each team could do, given the context in which they worked, and we found a way. So, I encourage you to consider what you can do and let go of the "That would never work here" mentality that is so easy to fall into.

Being the annoying champion for the "right way" of working. Some people, instead of adopting a "That will never work here" mindset, swing the pendulum too far in the other direction. They want to work using the "one right way" to do discovery. I have news for you. There *is no* "one right way" to do discovery. All of the habits in this book can and should be adopted to match your team's preferences and needs. This book isn't designed to be recipes that should be followed to the T, but rather templates that should help you get started. Once you have a handle on how they work, you can and should adopt them to better meet your own needs. Especially when you're new to adopting continuous discovery habits, don't let *perfect* be the enemy of *good*. Instead, adopt a continuous-improvement mindset. If next week looks better than last week, you are on the right track.

Waiting for permission instead of starting with what is within your control. I've met dozens of teams who have never talked to customers because they believe they aren't allowed to. However, they regularly engage with customers outside of work. They work for a major bank, and most (if not all) of their friends have a bank account. They build sales software, and their best friend's dad works in sales. They work on hospital badge systems, and they have three clinicians in their extended family. Don't let perfect be the enemy of good. Get started by talking to anyone who is like your customers. Iterate from there.

CHAPTER FIFTEEN

WHAT'S NEXT?

Congratulations! You've made it to the end of the book. However, this doesn't have to be the end of your *Continuous Discovery Habits* journey. I know it can be hard to translate what you read in a book to your own work, so I've collected a number of resources to support you while you continue your journey.

Subscribe to the Product Talk monthly newsletter. Every month, we release two long-form articles about continuous discovery. One month, we might highlight the work of real-world product teams putting *Continuous Discovery Habits* into practice. The next, we might publish a deep-dive, how-to article to help you hone your craft. Our goal with every article is to give you actionable insights that you can put into practice the same day. Sign up at ProductTalk.org.

Join the Continuous Discovery Habits membership community. We learn best in community. If you want to surround yourself with like-minded peers who are also investing in their continuous discovery habits, come join us. Membership includes monthly community calls in which you can connect with like-minded peers and the Product Talk coaches, fireside chats with product people who are seeing success putting the continuous discovery habits into practice, access to the Worthy Reads library, and much more. Learn more at: Members.ProductTalk.org.

Join a Master Class: Throughout the year, we host live Master Classes designed to help you develop the continuous discovery habits covered in this book. These courses include live instruction with me, are limited to small groups so that you have plenty of time to get your questions answered, and feature lots of hands-on, small-group activities so that you can apply what you are learning while also connecting with like-minded peers.

Join a skills deep-dive course. We offer several Deep-Dive courses that go deep in one of the continuous discovery habits. Want to hone your skill in story-based interviewing? Our Continuous Interviewing course was designed to get you hands-on practice. Not sure how to structure the opportunity space? Our Opportunity Mapping course teaches you how to map out the opportunity space step by step. Our Deep-Dive courses are designed to get you deliberate practice with a core discovery skill. Explore all the options at Learn.ProductTalk.org

Hire a Product Talk coach. Want more one-on-one help? Reach out to learn about our coaching options. Send me an email at teresa@producttalk.org.

Can you take a minute to help other product people?

Reading a book takes time. Many people decide whether a book is worth the investment by reading reviews. Would you mind taking a few minutes to review this book on Amazon or your favorite book site? Your opinion can make a difference. I would greatly appreciate it, and I know other product folks would as well.

As a thank-you, I have collected my list of recommended books here: amazon.com/shop/ttorres

ACKNOWLEDGMENTS

If this book has taught you anything, I hope it's that good products are created when the creators infuse their process with continuous feedback. That was especially true for this book.

The content in this book was developed and honed over the past seven years as I helped hundreds of product trios adopt continuous discovery habits. This book would not have been possible without those teams' curiosity, enthusiasm, and engagement. They asked insightful questions that pushed me to find better answers. They made it clear when an activity simply wasn't useful or sustainable. They persevered in the face of tough organizational challenges, helping me identify where the methods needed to get simpler. Every team that I have worked with has influenced this book in some way. So, to each of you, thank you! I love what we have created together.

I've been fortunate to have two collaborators who have pushed my thinking and kept me honest. I want to thank Hope Gurion and Jeff Merrell for their major contributions to the development of the ideas in this book.

Hope Gurion has been a client, a partner, and a friend. As a client, her feedback helped me see what I could uniquely offer to the world. As a partner, she's helped me expand Product Talk's coaching capacity and has made invaluable contributions to the curriculum. As a friend, she was a sounding board when this book was just a half-baked idea, supported me throughout its writing, and provided valuable feedback as a reviewer.

Jeff Merrell, my co-instructor at Northwestern, has been an amazing thought partner as we've worked to bring this curriculum to HR practitioners and organizational-change agents through the Masters in Learning and Organizational Change program. Translating these ideas for a broader business audience and getting a non-product person's perspective from Jeff has helped me develop and hone the ideas in this book. Not to mention his thoughtfulness, kindness, and unwavering support have been invaluable.

I want to thank Marty Cagan for his kind words in the Foreword, for his enthusiasm for my work, for the many referrals he has sent my way, for the critical feedback he provided when reviewing this book, and for the inspiring role he has played in developing the practice of product management. Marty, the product world is better for you. Thank you.

Martin Eriksson has been an incredible supporter of my work over the years, giving me several opportunities to speak at Mind the Product events, and was one of my trusted reviewers as I put the finishing touches on this book. Martin, your enthusiasm for the product community is infectious, and your feedback was invaluable. Thank you.

Petra Wille, who released an excellent book a few months before me, has been an incredible guide. She helped me navigate the self-publishing process, answered a million questions, and cheered me on as I finalized this book. Petra, I am so glad that we managed to write our books during the tumultuous year that was 2020 and that it brought us together. Your generosity has been bountiful. Thank you.

Melissa Suzuno, my blog editor and all-around content-marketing consultant, has been invaluable in making this book a reality. She edited and re-edited again and again. She highlighted where I needed examples or where my language wasn't clear. She taught me when to spell out numbers versus when to use numerals (even if I still get it wrong most of the time). And in a pivotal moment, she encouraged me to stay true to the book that I wanted to write. She was also instrumental in helping me to collect, write, and edit many of the customer stories that appear both in this book and in our "Product in Practice" series on Product Talk. Melissa, thank you for all of your support as this book came to fruition.

I wrote this book over the course of 2020. For the last 7 months of that year and into the first quarter of 2021, 58 product people have given me feedback through my Early Readers program as I wrote each chapter. They helped me understand what was working, what needed more work, and, most importantly, reminded me who I was writing this book for. Adam Cox, Alastair Lee, Alex Jacquet, Aneesha Govil, Anthony Sullivan, Cara Gaynor, Carl Harris, Cedric Constant, Chitraleka Creta, Chris Holmes, Chris Mercuri (who also wrote the opening Foreword), Cormac McLoughlin, Daria Fenske, Dominique Jost, Doug Simpson, Eirik Somerville, Eliane Pohl, Emily Tate, Flavio H.C. Freitas, Frank Lagendijk, Gale Robins, Gisela Souto Nogueira, Gustavo Goldenberg, Hana Vojáková, Jeremy Saenz, Kacy Schwartz, Karthik Natarajan, Kathy Bruder, Lars Böhnke, Lars Haßler, Lauren Nham, Lisa Orr, Matt LeMay, Maureen Eibeler, Megan Bruce, Michal Voják, Mustafa Al-Qinneh, Nandita Gokhale, Nik Laufer-Edel, Oliver Winter, Pat Boonyarittipong, Pete Anderson, Philipp Krehl, Reza Shirazi, Richard Hiscutt, Ruth Guthoff-Recknagel, Samantha Jacobs, Sarah Crispin, Shalini Kadaveru, Shobhit Chugh, Simon Diegmann, Sonja Alberdina Martin, Stephanie May, Sumi Thaiveettil, Tom Kazer, Tom Kerwin, Vikas Sah, Yelena Cope, thank you for all of your feedback and support as I wrote this book.

And finally, I want to thank Rick Gaudette, my partner in life, who learned way more about continuous discovery than he ever thought he would. As I wrote this book, he rode alongside me on the daily rollercoaster that is writing a book and supported me every step of the way.

Printed in the USA
CPSIA information can be obtained
at www.ICGtesting.com
LVHW051346051123
763097LV00004BA/396